Wild Embrace

CONNECTING
TO THE WONDER
OF IRELAND'S
NATURAL WORLD

Anja Murray is an ecologist, environmental policy analyst and broadcaster, familiar to many as a presenter of *Eco Eye* on RTÉ 1 and with her weekly *Nature File* on RTÉ lyric fm. Through these and her radio documentaries she explores the challenges facing the natural environment in Ireland through the perspective of what can be done to effect positive solutions.

Working in the NGO sector, with communities, state agencies, and youth groups, Anja has been pioneering innovative and collaborative approaches to nature conservation in Ireland for more than 20 years.

Wild

Embrace

CONNECTING
TO THE WONDER
OF IRELAND'S
NATURAL WORLD

Anja Murray

HACHETTE
BOOKS
IRELAND

First published in 2023 by Hachette Books Ireland

Copyright © Anja Murray

A CIP catalogue record for this title is available from the British Library.

ISBN 978 1 39971 189 0
Typeset in 11.5pt Adobe Garamond Pro
Interior design and typesetting by Cathal O'Gara
Interior illustrations by Jane Carkill

Printed and bound in Great Britain by Clays Ltd, Elcograf S.p.A.

Hachette Books Ireland policy is to use papers that are natural,
renewable and recyclable products and made from wood grown
in sustainable forests. The logging and manufacturing processes
are expected to conform to the environmental regulations of
the country of origin.

Hachette Books Ireland
8 Castlecourt Centre
Castleknock
Dublin 15, Ireland

A division of Hachette UK Ltd
Carmelite House, 50 Victoria Embankment, EC4Y 0DZ

www.hachettebooksireland.ie

Contents

Leisure

What is this life if, full of care,
We have no time to stand and stare?

No time to stand beneath the boughs
And stare as long as sheep or cows:

No time to see, when woods we pass,
Where squirrels hide their nuts in grass:

No time to see, in broad daylight,
Streams full of stars, like skies at night:

No time to turn at Beauty's glance,
And watch her feet, how they can dance:

No time to wait till her mouth can
Enrich that smile her eyes began?

A poor life this if, full of care,
We have no time to stand and stare.

by Welsh nature poet W.H. Davies, 1911

For Tito,

the best dog,

who has encouraged me in every adventure
and been by my side for every sentence written.

Embark on
your own joyful
journey of
discovery

Opening to the
Wild Embrace

WHEREVER we live, we are surrounded by wild things. Each autumn, globes of sweet-smelling ivy flowers erupt along walls and hedges, going unnoticed by us, but drawing in dozens of different bumblebees with drops of late-season nectar. Summer skies above city streets are speckled with swifts, gliding high on sickle-shaped wings that give them the power to fly faster than any other bird. Even the small clump of moss by the doorstep reveals its perfectly geometric design when examined closely. These things offer us a daily embrace from nature.

Perhaps you've noticed butterflies lingering on flowers and peered closer to look at their gorgeous colours. Have you ever wondered what they are doing there? They are probably warming their wings in the sunshine whilst guzzling sugary sustenance from each blossom they visit, drawing it up through a long appendage called a proboscis which works like a drinking straw. Each time they drink, they unfurl their proboscis into the heart of the flower, then roll it up again when they're done.

The last time you glimpsed a wild fox trotting down the road, did you notice the rich tones of its red fur and its discreet, wily gait? Maybe it was a male out foraging food for his mate, who stays tucked away in their sheltered den during March and April, suckling a brood of cubs. By June, cubs will be out playing and learning to cock their ears to the ground to listen for the sound of beetles and worms squirming about in the soil, only a scrape away from becoming a tasty snack.

Strolling down an urban laneway in summer, old walls may not be as grey as they seem. Cast your glance upwards and you might see elegant fractal-patterned ferns draping down beneath a leaky gutter; the succulent circular leaves of wall pennywort; colourful splodges of lichen; or towering bells of tubular foxglove flowers emerging from gaps. Each have exceeded the odds to seed themselves there, finding a nook in the wall where their special suite of evolutionary adaptations allows them to thrive.

For many of us, raised on television nature documentaries from far-flung places, nature is something exotic, out there. Yet all around us, wild stories are unfolding every day. The antics of some familiar Irish plants and animals are just as charismatic as those we see on television. Discovering them can be as easy as putting the phone away, looking up, peering closer, and being curious. Even within our immediate environment – on the bark of trees, in amongst the tangle of a hedge, emerging from flowery fields, and flying through the sky overhead – an endless variety of wild things are going about their lives.

Wild embrace is about awakening to the everyday nature in our midst. It's about tuning into the happenings taking place all around us; noticing how the ways of our native plants and animals are infinitely more interesting than we may have realised before.

'Wow' moments need not be confined to curated experiences or exotic places. A flicker of blue and yellow feathers on the garden wall leads us to discover that a pair of blue tits are busily feeding a brood of tiny, featherless chicks in a cavity not much bigger than our fist. Not only are the parents filling little beaks with caterpillars and worms, but they are also keeping the nest clean by removing tiny parcels of poo, which baby birds conveniently produce in neatly contained sacs. Each of us can experience daily awe – in the sublime patterning of a caterpillar munching on a bramble leaf at the side of the road; the cryptic camouflage of a furry white moth lingering on the white bark of a birch tree in the local park; or the swooping murmuration of a flock of starlings in winter.

When the scales fall from our eyes and we know what to look out for, glories like these can enrich our daily lives.

The Joy of Discovering

It is easy to tune out from the simple wonders around us,

dismiss them even as childish folly. Modern living provides us with no end of demands and distractions: busy schedules, smartphones, mental clutter. It can be difficult to slow down and take notice.

And there are so many environmental issues which can make us feel sad, fearful and powerless. But opening to the wild embrace can help us build emotional resilience, develop a deeper personal connection with the natural world, and empower us to engage positively with the critical issues.

Having worked in environmental education, policy and advocacy for decades, I am acutely aware of the plummeting populations of many of Ireland's most treasured birds, fish, butterflies and bees. Together with other ecologists, I have worked to convince decision-makers that action is urgently required. I thought that when the right civil servants, business leaders and politicians understood the full extent of the challenges facing Ireland's natural environment, and were presented with practical, evidence-based solutions, then policies and practices would be altered in response. But meeting after meeting, year after year, it became excruciating to witness so little being done to save our wild species. The laws protecting our most precious wildlife were routinely ignored. I began to understand that something fundamental is amiss. There had to be an explanation as to why people weren't listening.

When I delivered workshops to community groups, schoolteachers or local authority staff, highlighting the plight of bumblebees, wild birds and aquatic animals, people often told me afterwards that they felt totally overwhelmed. Most hadn't realised that things were so bad. They felt distressed and helpless upon hearing these stories. I saw that there is a bigger challenge facing us all. Banging people over the head with bad news, even while presenting solutions, won't change how we as a society behave towards the natural world. What is missing is a deeper emotional connection with nature.

Meanwhile, around 2011, after a dozen years of intense involvement in environmental policy and advocacy, I was beginning to experience burnout. I found that I rarely had time to soak up the sounds and colours of a woodland, lie low in long meadows listening for grasshoppers, or explore mountain valleys and wild Atlantic shores, even though these are the activities that nourish and sustain me. I was so immersed in battles for conservation that I forgot to nurture my own connection with wild nature – the very thing that had propelled me into the work that had become my life.

Then, prompted by a spate of grief and loss, I began to discover the healing power of wild places. I went regularly to skim stones on an overgrown riverbank near home and discovered kingfishers nesting on the opposite bank. My curiosity about bees and willow trees and sparrows was reignited. My little everyday adventures in nature became a lifeline.

In the years since, I have managed to transform my own relationship with Ireland's natural world, exploring more, making time for regular immersion, learning every day, and working in television and radio to communicate as I learn. By re-awakening my own connection, I have found that I am able to approach life with a fresher, more positive perspective. Cultivating curiosity and love has built up my emotional resilience, enhancing my abilities both to engage with personal challenges, and to work with others to bring about the policy changes that we still very much need.

I see now, more than I ever did before, that we are unlikely to truly respect, care for and defend that which we do not know and love. Spending time in nature has well-established links with positive environmental behaviours and attitudes.[1] For this reason, it is good to remind ourselves and each other about the power of the wild embrace.

This book brings together my love for and knowledge of Irish nature, in a celebration of what I call wild reverence. It offers an invitation for you, the reader, to cultivate a more direct relationship with everyday elements of the living world, embarking on your own joyful journey of discovery. Here is a guide to help you develop and nurture the skills you need to carry you on a lifelong adventure with the nature all around you.

Each of us
can actively
nurture hope

Connection

BREATHE in and feel molecules of oxygen swooshing into your lungs. Imagine looking up through the green leafy canopy of a tree and breathe again, deeply; or better still, go outside and gaze up into an actual tree, allowing the cast of green-hued light to enfold body and mind.

The oxygen in every breath we've ever taken comes from plants growing both on land and in the sea. To acknowledge this is an exercise in humility, a pathway to connection. Strengthening relationships with the natural world begins with each of us rekindling our own connections to the nature around us.

In Ireland, many of us are surrounded with opportunities to experience being out in wild places. We can listen to birdsong echoing in the dappled light of a wooded valley in spring; soak up the delicate beauty of swathes of primroses growing in a hedge bank; or ramble through late summer sunshine on heather-clad hills. Regular experiences in nature soothe our busy minds and can make us both healthier and happier.

These are the mental states that can equip us with emotional resilience, awaken empathy, and even cause us to recognise how deeply we are connected to each other and to everything else in the biosphere. It's not hard to see, therefore, that spending more time in nature can open us to the possibilities of living in better balance with the natural world.

Woodland Wonder

Growing up in the beautiful Wicklow hills with ample access to big old trees, intriguing woodlands and sandy lakeshores, I have always been somewhat feral – delighting in the patterns of veins on a leaf, the textures of flower petals, and the iridescent colours on a butterfly wing. And I have always been aware of how good nature makes me feel. Recent advances in science have corroborated what many of us know intuitively: that being in nature has a powerfully positive impact on our mental well-being.

During a particularly difficult period of my life, when I was caring for my terminally ill mother, I found myself cast adrift into an overwhelming numb sadness. The emotional distress triggered some alarming physical symptoms, including a strange allergic reaction that landed me in an ambulance and overnight in an intensive care unit. As soon as I got out, I instinctively knew that I needed to get myself to my favourite hazel wood, a small parcel of wild woodland nestled in a forgotten corner of west Cavan.

I craved the reassurance of being bathed in dappled light, and the soothing soundtrack of the rust brown river running over pebble banks and gurgling around boulders. The familiarity and safety of a riotous green tangle drew my mind and my heart out of their grieving states, back into the wild natural world. We all know that feeling at a familiar lakeside walk or woodland, when our shoulders drop down our backs by several inches and stress dissipates in the breeze. We regain a sense of ease and perspective; we breathe deeper and feel calmer. We 'come to our senses' and become more present in the world.

I don't own the woods that I describe above. I didn't grow up near them, yet I feel very much at home there. Whatever the time of year, I am mesmerised by the light, and by the many textures and sounds of the place. Over the years, I have gradually come to know most of the nooks and crannies of this small green and golden realm. I know where the swathes of bluebells and wood anemones carpet the ground in spring. I watch in awe as they're lit up by beams of morning sunlight pouring through the canopy. When the trees begin to bud, they fill the scene with delicate, fresh potential. I feel reassurance emanating from the moss-covered branches and their covering of luminous ferns.

By midsummer there are occasional orchids, purple and white, poking their proud heads from openings between thickets of bramble. Delicate young saplings of hawthorn and hazel are nurtured by their woodland kin, linked through subterranean networks of mycorrhiza, the fungal webs that I can't see but know are there. In autumn, I look for tiny white toadstools, only a few millimetres tall, growing from leftover hazelnut shells split open by squirrels.

Each of these elements has become familiar because I spend time in this woodland regularly, quietly, often alone. It is one of the most captivating hideaways that I know, made more so by my familiarity with the place. The first time I wandered into these woods, I was delighted by my discovery, but each subsequent visit left me enamoured anew. In time, I came to crave the sight of the golden, delicately patterned bark of the hazel wands, and the fallen tree by the river where I often perch, surrounded by branches, leaves, ferns and green things growing as they please. This is where I return to when I need to return to myself.

In reality, this special place is an unassuming patch of woodland, tucked away on a steep slope between the bend of a river and two small country roads. It is not recognised, celebrated, designated as a nature reserve, or even visited by anyone else as far as I know. It's a place where everyday wild things live free: beautifully marked fritillary butterflies, perfectly camouflaged moths, tiny long-nosed shrews, a clan of badgers, elusive long-eared owls and cryptically coloured woodcocks; all of whom I see evidence of when I potter about here. Noticing their signs and trails absorbs me so much that I often lose my sense of time. Each time I visit I notice or learn something new. Without knowingly seeking it, I've come to this strong sense of connection through slowing down, observing details, and being open to the prompts and clues on offer.

Healing Nature

A great many discoveries in neuroscience and evolutionary psychology in recent years have revealed the physiological and psychological benefits of being in nature. We love to be in woodlands and lush meadows, surrounded by the soothing colours and patterns that nature has designed. Gentle rhythmic movements of tree leaves or tall grasses calm our senses, because we are genetically predisposed to feel relaxed in natural places. We are, after all, products of biological evolution and we have evolved, quite literally, in wild places. Modern humans are part of the biosphere. We have been shaped by our relationships with wild plants and animals.

Biologists have established, for example, that human vision has evolved to be sensitive to green and red, an advantage for hunter-gatherers scanning from a distance for ripe fruit and useful vegetation. By contrast, bees are not so good at seeing red, but have adapted the ability to see ultraviolet light, useful for collecting nectar from flowers. Using ultraviolet patterns on their petals, flowers literally signpost the way down to the nectar within.

Because we have evolved as one component of a complex biosphere, it makes perfect sense that our mental well-being[2] is improved when we are in a natural environment. Our minds have not evolved to feel comfortable amongst grey shades of concrete, straight lines of tarmacadam[3] or the bustle of car traffic.

Recent advances in psychology are uncovering how time in nature[4] improves cognitive ability, increases the production of serotonin, induces kind behaviour, aids clear thinking, and improves our overall levels of happiness. Just 15 to 20 minutes in the natural world – connecting with it through the senses of sight, hearing, smell and touch – is found to significantly lower blood pressure, pulse rate, and cortisol or stress hormone levels. A corollary of this is that habitual separation from nature can lead to aggression, irritability, stress, and even physical illness. Time in nature is at the heart of our physical and mental well-being. It is no wonder that many of us are innately driven to spend time outdoors.

Amazingly, plants have been found to release organic compounds called phytoncides, which boost the human immune system by increasing production of a particular kind of white blood cell that responds to viruses. Based on this knowledge, it's not surprising that a multitude of studies have shown that recovery times from illness are shorter with exposure to nature. In Ireland, following international evidence, GPs in different parts of the country have begun prescribing time in nature as a treatment for stress-related ailments.

Because we are predisposed to feel more relaxed in natural environments, a growing number of psychotherapists meet their clients in outdoor settings, an approach called nature-based therapy. One of the phenomena that such psychotherapists apply is 'soft fascination', which refers to how watching movement – such as reeds swaying on a lakeshore or leaves fluttering in a breeze – has a soothing effect on our brains and our nervous systems. Natural occurrences that attract our attention with movement, especially rhythmic movement, draw us out from overthinking, to a more present and relaxed state of mind. Therapists describe an expanded sense of self that results from being in nature. This expanded state provides a healthier context within which to discuss difficult emotions.

Alongside the measurable therapeutic and medical applications of prescribing time in nature, there are a myriad of everyday benefits that don't require studies to convince us of their existence. Observing the details of beautiful natural patterns, like those in a leaf or a damselfly wing, both stimulates and soothes. The more we look, the more curious we become, and the more we wish to discover. This is a feedback loop that brings us ever closer to joyful presence.

But being 'in nature' is not as simple as it seems. Studies have shown that the quality of the natural environment matters. Subjects who spend time in more biodiverse settings with a variety of natural components experience stronger and more lasting mental health benefits. This has implications for the places we choose to go to when we are taking the time to be in nature, especially if we are seeking to improve our well-being as a result.[5]

If you are heading off for a few hours in the woods, both the setting and how we behave when get there make a big difference to our experience. In a mixed woodland with a good variety of tree species and a healthy mix of different tree ages, sizes and textures, there will also be a healthy variety of flowering plants. Here a vivid chorus of birdsong will echo through the woodland layers, while delicate birch and deep green spindle trees catch the beams of light falling through the canopy overhead. Leaves might be soft like hazel or hard like holly, rough like elm or smooth and lobed like oak. Ferns of different shapes decorate fallen logs, and wild honeysuckle weaves its way around branches.

Biodiverse habitats such as these tend to have a more soothing impact on our nervous systems than do monocultures, such as intensively farmed fields or sitka spruce plantations. Our instinctive affinity with diversity is deeply encoded. To experience the benefits of biodiversity, we can go to native woodlands to try a bit of 'forest bathing'. This involves being still, and mindfully absorbing the sights, smells and sounds of a woodland. Staying quiet and present, we can tune into the physiological effects of sensory connection with the nature all around us.

But if we go forest bathing in an industrially managed conifer forest, among uniform rows of the same species of tree where diversity is much diminished, the mental benefits are not as far-reaching. Many of the elements which anchor and connect us are absent in a dark plantation of spruce trees.

As we go about cultivating our connection with nature, it is worth remembering how the quality of the environment impacts the benefits we gain from our experiences in the outdoors. Monoculture farmland, manicured parkland lawns, and neatly planted borders of exotic evergreen bushes might be better than the concrete jungle, but they are only a pale shadow of the rich diversity of natural habitats.

Challenging Disempowerment

News of environmental collapse and species on the brink of extinction, here in Ireland as well as across the world, is clearly distressing. It is entirely logical to feel despair about the current state of the world. Knowing that the policy responses have to date been insufficient to affect the scale of change that is needed causes us to feel despondent and cynical. No wonder we can feel overwhelmed, disempowered and disinclined to hold any hope about the future.

These ubiquitous emotional states are now named 'climate-' and 'eco-anxiety'. They describe a decline in mental health related to the global climate crisis and environmental degradation. Feeling guilty about the small contributions of our own behaviour to climate pollution is another aspect of this.

Sometimes we must turn off from the facts in order to protect our mental health, but this can lead us into a cycle of avoidance and an even deeper disconnect. Succumbing to avoidance, cynicism or feelings of guilt stifles our ability to think critically about problems, to imagine creative solutions, and to respond appropriately (or even respond at all). Rekindling our connections to nature, as described in the following chapters, and taking positive action can help manage distressing feelings associated with eco-anxiety.

Each of us can actively nurture hope that things will change for the better. I like to think of the fundamentals of hope as a three-legged stool – where each respective leg represents wonder, knowledge and action. Without all three legs, the stool topples over and we fall into despair, burnout or cynicism.

The wild embrace offers easy ways to access nature as an antidote to overwhelm. I propose a fresh perspective from which to perceive nature – including everyday details about butterflies, wildflowers and birds that are commonplace. My goal is to instil in readers the habit of pausing more often, looking more closely; peeling away the filters and inhibitions that tend to quash curiosity. In opening your eyes and your minds to even the most familiar wild plants and animals, you can access a never-ending source of discovery, wonder and delight. This is the wild embrace.

But before we take a more detailed look at some of the surprising goings on in your local woodlands, river or meadow, and how to discover their joys for yourself, we need to go back in time. Join me on a short detour into our past, to explore some of the historical and cultural forces that have shaped our relationships with the natural world. Understanding how we have become so disconnected will aid us on our journey back to connection.

Invitations to the Wild Embrace

❦ Explore some places near where you live to discover elements of wild nature there. For example, a small pocket of broadleaved woodland, an accessible lakeshore, or a piece of forgotten waste ground. Go to your chosen places regularly to observe changes in plant and animal life across the seasons.

❦ Get a lightweight pocket notebook in which you can write nature notes and observations, as well as questions to look up later. Keeping a record of what you learn and discover helps you to remember and to compare notes from season to season.

❦ When you next take a walk, slow right down and look all around – at the plants growing from old walls, or up into the tree canopy overhead. Take time to observe subtle details. Rather than feeling self-conscious or childish, be brazenly curious.

❦ Lie back in a meadow or a native woodland and quietly pay attention to the sights, sounds and smells of life all around. Observe how this makes you feel. Repeat this exercise regularly.

The ultimate
deity was the
earth goddess

Reclaiming the Past

WALKING through a native Irish woodland at any time of year is an enthralling experience. Limbs of enormous oak trees mingle with tall pine, creating a cathedral-like ambiance. A rich mosaic of hazel and hawthorn lives beneath. We are immersed in layers of life, breathing deep, surrounded by the singing of great tits, wagtails and blackbirds, the drone of bees and hoverflies, and the rustling of leaves.

Deciduous woodlands once covered almost every hill, valley and plain across Ireland. Only where lakes, bogs and marshes exist do the woodlands naturally yield. After the ice sheets had retreated in Ireland about 11,000 years ago, pioneering birch, willow and hazel led the way, followed by vast woodlands of oak, elm, pine, alder and ash. Thanks to the water-laden air masses carried in from the Atlantic Ocean, our native woodlands are padded out with moisture-loving mosses, ferns, liverworts and lichens, claiming every available surface.

For thousands of years, pine martens and red squirrels

could clamber along branches and weave their way through treetops all the way from coast to coast. Ample populations of small animals, such as wood mice and shrews, provided plentiful sustenance for eagles, sparrowhawks, goshawks and long-eared owls. Wolves roamed widely, maintaining balance in the ecosystem, as all top predators do. For the first several thousand years of human habitation here, these woodlands were all that people knew. Our culture is borne of the woods; we are originally woodland inhabitants.

How we interact with nature is determined by the legacy of previous generations, extending back hundreds, if not thousands, of years. Each new wave of settlers that arrived to this island at the edge of Europe revolutionised our relationship to the land. We are fortunate that the thread of cultural reverence for the natural world has not been completely severed; we still retain some of the understandings enshrined in belief systems that existed long before our current medley of influences.

It is worth looking to the past for glimmers of the connection that our ancestors had with the natural world. Throughout Ireland, we are fortunate to be surrounded by monuments built by ancient civilisations. From megalithic tombs such as Newgrange, aligned with winter solstice, to the castles of conquerors, historic places give us a continuity with the past, and can also provide us with reminders for the future, in terms of what we ourselves are leaving for the generations to come.

Ireland is rich in ancient beliefs, which have wended their way through time in customs and folklore. Wild plants and animals have been integral to our stories, songs, language and place names, and have given context to our culture. Romantic writers and creators in the 1920s picked up resonant threads of ancient Irish culture to generate a portrayal of post-independence Irish identity that reconnected us to heroic elements of our past. We can pick up threads from the same ancient source now, in how we envision a viable, ecologically sound future that reflects the importance of wild places and kindred plants and animals.

Incorporating a longer perspective, which stretches backward as well as forward, is necessary if we are to cultivate the shift in values needed to preserve that which is infinitely precious – the wild nature that thrives in a healthy natural environment.

The First People

The first people to arrive in Ireland were Mesolithic hunter-gatherers who ventured here from the east in wooden dugout canoes[6] over 12,000 years ago, settling along coasts, lakes and rivers. Their lives were enmeshed with the wild plants and animals in their environment and tempered by the variable bounty of seasonal offerings. They had impressive knowledge and skill for gathering, processing and preserving wild foods and materials for daily life.

They built homes with hazel and hide, and were familiar with the characteristics and multiple uses of thousands of plant fibres, animal carcasses and rock types. Their diet was rich in plant tubers, leaves, fungi, wild fruits and nuts, and they also utilised wild herbs and fungi as medicine. They wove baskets for everyday use and crafted watertight containers from animal skins. They knew how to make glue and thread from the sinews and bones of the animals they hunted. For at least 4,000 years, Mesolithic people lived directly from wild resources and left almost no trace of themselves in the landscape.

Prior to the arrival of human life, there are no traces of wild boars in Ireland. It seems that Mesolithic people carried them across the sea in dugout boats. Wild boar was a species that adapted readily to the wooded environment and thereafter supplied a continuous source of meat, bone for making tools, and hides for shelter and clothing. There is evidence to suggest that wild boars were hunted at low levels to ensure the population was not unduly diminished. Mesolithic people also lived alongside brown bears and wolves, the top mammalian predators of temperate wild woodland habitats in this part of the world.

We know that hunter-gatherers lived near lakes and rivers where big fleshy sturgeon, salmon, trout and eel were abundant and easily caught. They used hazel rods to make fish traps, catching migrating fish travelling downstream after spawning, or trapping fish in tidal estuaries. When excavations began for the construction of the Convention Centre on Dublin's quays, archaeologists discovered a Mesolithic fish trap woven from hazel. Dating and analysing the hazel rods, they determined that all the rods were of a similar girth and age, which tells us that hunter-gatherers were harvesting hazel in such a way as to produce a crop of rods with similar diameters every few years. Rather than living from hand to mouth, these hunter-gatherers had detailed knowledge of their environment, and were managing wild habitats in subtle ways to maintain continually regenerating harvests of the materials they depended on.

Hunter-gatherers did not farm, use metals, or build lasting monuments, but they had an intricate understanding of their environment and how to make the most of the wild resources available to them. These were not savages, but rather people whose cultural traditions carried an understanding through the generations about the long-term implications of over-exploitation. We have no way of knowing their creation stories, rituals, beliefs, social hierarchies, music or art, but we do have some clues about the nature of Mesolithic societies.

From excavated bones, which scientists can date and analyse, we know that hunter-gatherers in Ireland ate birds of prey: ospreys, owls, goshawks and peregrine falcons. The flesh of raptors such as these is neither tasty nor worth the calorific return for the hunting effort, so academics have deduced that our hunter-gatherer ancestors ate them not for nutrition, but to absorb the prowess of those they recognised as masters of hunting.[7] In animistic belief, everything in the world is infused with spirit so that by eating an owl, one could absorb its powerful night vision. From this perspective, a peregrine falcon is imbued with a spirit of speed which could be transferred to those consuming its flesh. In the animistic world view, the characteristics of every living thing are considered, recognised and valued.

Traditionally, indigenous peoples have intimate knowledge of the land. Stories and ceremonies attest to wise usage of natural resources in order to ensure continued bounty. The fact that hunter-gatherers lived for such a very long time here in Ireland would suggest that they too had similar approaches to living.

We have inherited the colonial perspective that hunter-gatherers were 'primitive', a bias that extends to the indigenous hunter-gatherer cultures still in existence today. As we witness the degradation of nature everywhere, there is a great deal to learn from the sustaining environmental practices of indigenous cultures and remaining hunter-gatherer societies.

The First Farmers
The Neolithic period in Ireland, from about 4,500 BC, began when the first farmers came here[8], bringing with them the knowledge that spread a technological revolution across the land. This period saw people ploughing the soil to plant cereal crops and rearing domesticated animals for the first time, thus

creating food surpluses. Woodlands were cleared with stone axes to make room for crops and grazing herds of cattle and sheep. A whole new level of control was being exerted upon the land. The first farmers didn't have formal fields: animals such as cows, pigs and goats would roam in the woodlands, while clearings among the woodland canopy were made in order to grow barley, rye and emmer wheat.

These animals and crops were new to Irish shores, brought in by new settlers and a novel culture. But traditions fused, and the clearings made for these new crops created edges where woodland meets open ground. Woodland edges are where elder, hawthorn, blackthorn, dog rose, honeysuckle and wild strawberries grow, plants of wild margins, which today remain the plants of hedgerow habitats. Coinciding with the clearances, wild fruits such as blackberries, sloes, rosehips, haws and crab apples would have increased in abundance.

Farming did not replace the gathering of wild foods, which continued for thousands of years yet. Blackberries were one of the few sources of sweetness in the days before sugar and were thus likely celebrated. Elderberries would have been valuable for rich flavour and high vitamin content. Haws – the fruit of hawthorn trees – were harvested and processed for the fleshy outer layer of the fruit, high in vitamin C and a tonic for the heart. As farming spread, woodlands remained a significant source of food and building materials. Evidence from continental Europe tells us that people at this time were also using medicinal plants and fungi, including using particular fungi with antibiotic, anti-inflammatory and antiviral properties.[9]

As farming spread across Ireland, so did the Neolithic custom of building megalithic tombs for communal burial. There are more than 1,500 court cairns, portal tombs, passage tombs and wedge tombs still in place today on hilltops across the country.[10] They are traces of a Neolithic culture that left its imprint on the land, with monuments and alterations to landscapes as woodlands were gradually cleared to create grassy pastures for farm animals and open ground for growing cereal crops.

Many Neolithic tombs were oriented to the sun's rays on the summer and winter solstices (the longest and shortest days of the year), and the spring and autumn equinoxes (the midpoints between the longest and shortest days). The Neolithic passage tomb at Newgrange in County Meath, for example, faces the rising sun on the winter solstice, the only time each year when the sun's rays penetrate into the burial chamber inside the tomb. At the Neolithic site at Lough Gur in County Limerick, there is a stone circle aligned with the summer solstice. At other sites, dawn sunlight strikes the inside of the tomb twice per year, at the spring and autumn equinox. Such deliberate solar alignments demonstrate a precise knowledge of astronomy and perhaps reverence for the sun.

As well as being important markers of time and the changing seasons, on which the cycles of hunting, gathering and farming depend, it has been suggested that capturing the sun's rays on these particular days indicates a reverence for the interaction between the sun and the earth, the source of all fertility and growth. That the bones of prominent ancestors were interred in these tombs suggests a complex set of beliefs and customs relating to the sun, the seasons, the cosmos, the passing of time and the possibility of an afterlife.

Pagan beliefs based on the natural cycles of nature and the movement of the earth around the sun help to explain the great effort that went into constructing the enormous, chambered cairns of our Neolithic ancestors. Rituals may have been performed to mark seasonal transitions, such as the pagan festivals of Imbolc (February 1st), Bealtaine (May 1st), Lughnasa (August 1st), and Samhain (October 31st–November 1st).

Archaeologists have also unearthed stone axes from this time that are too big to be of practical use. These beautifully rounded and polished implements are thought to have been made for ritual or ceremonial purposes, symbolising the power that these tools could wield over the environment, celebrating people's new-found ability to change the landscape.

We have other glimpses too of how Neolithic people perceived their place in nature. Because the land produced new life, it was thought of as female in gender and the ultimate deity was the earth goddess. The sun is also needed to produce new life, and was thought of as male in gender, represented by the sun god. Each king represented the sun god and was 'married' to a conceptual earth goddess, his role to maintain harmony between people and the land. Damaging the land was disrespecting the earth goddess, who in response might unleash disasters such as storms, droughts, floods, plagues or war.

Several 'bog bodies' discovered in Ireland's midland bogs are well preserved young adult males from the Neolithic period. They were relatively well-groomed and, based on the absence of callouses on their hands or scratches on their fingernails, they were likely to have been men of nobility, probably kings. It is thought that these kings were sacrificed when the natural world appeared to be out of balance, the consequences of which might entail loss of fertility, drought or famine. The king was held responsible, having failed in his duty to create balance between people and the land, which was also seen as an affront to the goddess. Sacrificing the king and depositing his body in the bog was believed to restore equilibrium.

Wet places that are neither land nor water, bogs were where the veil between this world and the otherworld was perceived to be at its thinnest; thus they were deemed appropriate places to leave the bodies of kings, sacrificed as offerings to appease the earth goddesses and entice the return of health, fertility and prosperity.

We do not know exactly the beliefs and rituals of Neolithic

people, and all of this is a speculative reconstruction. However, it is a reconstruction informed by the legends and oral histories that have survived, and evidence pieced together from archaeological finds. This retelling of the spiritual beliefs of those times has a resonance for today. In essence, these stories reveal an acknowledgement that humanity is entirely dependent on the natural word for its sustenance and survival; that the fertility of the land is often beyond what we can control; and that the people who lived in Ireland more than 5,000 years ago had a deep reverence for 'Mother Earth'. They had deep-rooted cultural practices to embed the belief that when their leaders failed to maintain balance between human society and nature, the consequences would be catastrophic.

In the 6,000 years since the Neolithic period, the gradual process of taming Ireland's once wild landscapes continued, as technologies developed and belief systems changed. Some of the core values from this period have been retained, morphing with time and being adapted to fit with each new culture that arrived.

For example, it is thought that the Christian figure now known as St Brigid, whose feast day is celebrated on February 1st, is likely a Christian re-interpretation of one of the earth goddesses, Bríde, with origins in the Neolithic. St Brigid's Day is also known as Imbolc. On this day, some of the passage tombs from this period are illuminated by the rising sun. This marked the end of the earth's winter sleep and the beginning of spring, the turning point at which new life begins to awake from dormancy, when seeds were sown for the year ahead.

In the following chapter, we explore how history unfolded to create the landscapes familiar to us today, so that we might understand what is to be done to restore nature's balance. Because diverse native woodlands are the natural climax habitat of most of Ireland, understanding their history is key to their future.

Invitations to the Wild Embrace

❦ Visit one of the over a thousand megalithic tombs dotted across Ireland. If possible, go on one of the days of their solar alignments, such as summer solstice or autumn equinox, to see the light entering their inner chambers as it has since these monuments were built.

❦ When you look out over the landscape, imagine what it might have looked like to the hunter-gatherers who lived in Ireland 10,000 years ago.

❦ Mark the transition of the seasons, and research how auspicious times of year were celebrated in ancient times.

❦ Ask elderly neighbours or relatives if they have memories or stories about celebrating Brigid's Day on February 1st.

Irish chieftains
kept wolves
as pets

Taming

TO understand the taming of the Irish landscape we shall first return to an ancient oak woodland, where moss-covered branches of sprawling trees reach out in every direction, draped in perfectly luscious ferns that dangle down from overhead. Saplings of holly, hawthorn and hazel position their leaves to soak up the light that pours down through the canopy. Underneath, the ground is covered in a tangle of different textures and shades of green. Brambles clamber over a messy mosaic of fallen logs and leaves. Elegant bouquets of woodrush dot the scene. Big rocky boulders are covered in thick cushions of soft moss. Delicate flowering towers of wild orchids mingle with the lily-like shape of 'lords and ladies'. Big soft mounds of moss are scattered throughout like beanbags.

Every nook and cranny is literally brimming with life. These woodlands are so saturated in moist oceanic air that they are also known as temperate rainforests. Tree bark is coloured in with lichens, speckled, sprayed and splodged.

Deeper crevices on old trees provide shelter for caterpillars, moths, ants, beetles, shield-bugs and many other insects. Expertly camouflaged treecreepers use their feathered wings to steady their steps as they walk in circles round the tree trunks, picking out their invertebrate dinners with perfectly adapted beaks.

The alarming screech of jays and the rhythmical tapping of spotted woodpeckers solo over the chorus of more melodious wrens, tits, robins and chaffinches. Millions of tiny flying insects provide a gentle drone. Each organism has a role in this ecosystem. Small birds eat caterpillars and save the tree leaves from annihilation. Jays eat acorns and inadvertently help new oak saplings to establish. Woodpeckers tap holes into tree trunks, claiming territory with the percussive sound while also mining for beetles and grubs to eat. The holes they leave behind create roosting sites for bats, who feed on moths and hoverflies. This is but one example of how several species' life strategies knit together, fine-tuned by millions of years of evolution, in which individual components have come to depend on one another.

It can be hard to imagine how only a few thousand years ago scenes like this covered the entirety of this island.[11]

But now, almost every element of wild nature in Ireland has been tamed. Rivers that for millennia were teeming with life, abundant with populations of salmon, trout and sturgeon, have been straightened, dredged and dammed. Upland areas are heavily grazed by sheep, leaving little room for the wild plants and birds that once thrived. Even our national parks are small by European standards and are overgrazed, planted with commercial conifers, infested with invasive species and denied the conditions necessary for healthy habitats to thrive.

Yet there are still places across Ireland teeming with wildlife, where we have opportunities to cultivate a relationship with wild things, even though, in ecological terms, we know that we have lost a great deal and that many species are in trouble today.

Because there is still time to restore ecosystems to a healthy state, it is necessary to understand the baseline and how we have dropped so far below it, so that we have the capacity to imagine the natural wealth that it is still possible for us to help renew.

Early Woodland Clearances

Land that was originally opened up by the early farmers of the Neolithic period, to make place for crops and domesticated animals, often regenerated back to woodland again.

But when people figured out how to make metal in the Bronze Age, which began about 4,500 years ago, the clearances accelerated. Bronze axes were far more effective at cutting through trees than stone axes had been. Huge quantities of timber were needed to fire furnaces to make metal tools, so there was a double incentive to cut down wild woodlands.

For thousands of years, woodlands continued to be cleared, although open ground was still surrounded by wild woods. Clearances accelerated during the Iron Age, which began about 500 BC, when even greater quantities of timber were needed to smelt iron ore. This new technology ushered in new levels of prosperity that in turn created greater demand for agricultural produce.

During the early medieval period, from about the fifth century AD, more and more people moved into towns. Open fields with cattle, hay meadows and cereal crops began to dominate the landscape, interspersed with wild woodlands, wet floodplain marshes and vast expanses of wet bog. In the eighth century a set of complex laws were laid down in writing. These are known as the Brehon Laws, in Irish called *Bretha Comaithcheasa*, which translates as the 'Laws of the Neighbourhood'. The Brehon Laws set out how people were expected to interact over issues such as hunting and fishing rights, and who was entitled to what share of the honey made by bees foraging on their land for nectar. The Brehon Laws are evidence of a collective desire to manage resources with sustainability in mind.

The Brehon Laws ranked trees according to their value and utility, allocating very high penalties for anyone causing damage to a high-ranking tree, specifically oak, ash, hazel, holly, crab apple, yew and Scots pine – the five *airig fedo*: 'nobles of the wood'. Oak was prized for its strong timber and crop of acorns each autumn, which fed domestic pigs through winter months. Hazel was valuable as a continuously regenerating building material, as well as for nutritious hazelnuts. Holly's evergreen leaves were cut and used as cattle fodder right up until recent times. Ash was considered noble for its wood, which is strong yet flexible. Both yew and Scots pine were also valued for their strong and durable timber. Crab apple was protected under the Brehon Laws as an important seasonal food source. Whoever caused harm to one of these noble trees was levied with a heavy penalty of two 'milch' cows (milking cows were the most valuable livestock) and a three-year-old heifer – a punitive fine indeed.

By the late medieval period, beginning in the mid-twelth century, Ireland's landscapes were dominated by agriculture but still rich with wild places: native deciduous woodlands full of wildlife and untamed rivers. People were still very much reliant on wild-caught fish, birds, roots, leaves, fruits and nuts, all harvested according to the seasons. Acorns and crab apples were fed to pigs. Gorse bushes were processed to feed to horses. Woven baskets were essential everyday utility items, made from both wild and cultivated willow, with each community having its own unique style and pattern of basketry.

People knew how and where to gather and prepare wild-growing medicinal plants to treat a range of ailments. Dyes for wool and linen were made using lichens, bark, nuts and leaves. Plant-based tannins were used to preserve leather. Cords and rope were made with straw and other plant materials. The essentials of daily life were harvested directly from the wild, so people in the medieval period would still have had an intimate understanding of their local environment and the seasonal patterns of wild plants and animals.

It is only in the past 200 years that so many of these skills have begun to disappear from common knowledge. As the direct connection between people and the land diminished, so did the perspective of being deeply entwined with the bounty of nature. People who continue these venerable traditions sustain that sense of connection to the landscape.

Basket-makers today, for example, have an impressive understanding of the varieties of willow that grow well here, how to grow them and when to harvest (after the first full moon of November). Many ancient crafts still survive. Wood turning, basket making, making hazel hurdles for fencing, extracting natural textile dyes from plants, weaving with plant fibres and wool, preparing plant-based cosmetics – each of these uses natural materials and ancient skills to make everyday necessities. Learning traditional crafts resurrects our connection to the wild, reminding us that people have always been inventive and resourceful, long before industrial processes or digital technology came about.

Religion and Colonialism

In the sixth century, when Ireland was a refuge for European

Christianity, Christian monks based themselves in monasteries in some of the most scenic parts of Ireland. They wrote beautiful poems celebrating the natural world and its cast of beloved wild birds, animals, wildflowers and trees, capturing the characters of each, as well as the patterns and cycles of the natural world. Age-old beliefs and customs originating in pre-Christian times were incorporated into Christian stories, allowing remnants to carry through to modern customs, though the messages were adapted to Christian teachings.

In the sixteenth century, however, Christianity was interpreted in such a way as to justify the colonial exploitation of many parts of the world. As Europeans became more and more exploitative in their behaviour, new Christian narratives were developed that gave credence to conquest and slavery. Colonialism caused environmental destruction on a scale never seen before, in Ireland and across the world. The prevalence of particularly conservative interpretations of Christianity transformed people's perception of their place in the natural world, as 'wild' was decreed ungodly.

The ample timber in Irish forests – used for building naval ships with which the British could colonise and defend new territories across the globe – was a sought-after resource for the growing British empire. In order to lay the moral foundations for the conquest of Ireland and clearance of the remaining woodlands, Irish people and culture were mocked and indigenous language, traditions and customs were oppressed.

For example, English manuscripts from the 1500s frequently describe the Irish as 'wilde' and savage, apparently able to sustain ourselves quite sufficiently on a diet of leaves and milk. Numerous references in plays and travelogues from this period describe the Irish as living on shamrocks, watercress and wild roots. An English doctor who published a pamphlet in 1680 on the virtues of a vegetarian diet cited the Irish as being 'swift of foot and nimble of strength', apparently because of our diet of leaves and roots. This derisive description of the native Irish being able to survive on a diet of wild plants and milk is the origin of our modern association with the shamrock, our national trademark.

By the year 1600, after only 50 years of Tudor conquest, woodland cover in Ireland was reduced to an estimated 12 per cent. Colonialisation continued through the 1600s, and the last great expanses of ancient woodland were cut down in this period. When Cromwell came to re-conquer Ireland in 1649, the objective was to clear the land of rebels and to civilise the country. This involved clearing the remaining wild woodlands, along with the wild wolves who inhabited them and the Irish rebels who tended to find refuge in woods. Some of the woodlands were simply burnt down so that Irish rebels would have nowhere left to hide from government troops.

To the native Irish, wolves had been respected as *mac tíre*, which directly translates as 'son of the land'. Irish chieftains kept wolves as pets. To the new settlers, however, wolves were seen as the last vestige of wildness and thus had to be exterminated. With characteristic efficiency, Cromwell set a generous bounty on the heads of wolves, and most were eliminated in just a few decades.

In the 1840s, when famine struck, evictions by landlords were commonplace. Landowners loyal to the British crown evicted tenants and replaced them with sheep, which at this point were becoming a valuable commodity. High levels of sheep stocking, especially across the uplands, obliterated layers of native wildlife, and continues to prevent regeneration of native woodlands in these areas, despite contemporary knowledge of the environmental benefits offered by natural woods and peatlands.

After a century of independence, little has been done to heal the ecological wounds of colonial legacy. We have achieved forest cover of only 11 per cent (compared to a European average of 36 per cent) and only a tiny proportion of this is native or semi-natural woodland.

Deciduous woodland is the natural climax vegetation of Ireland. There is an onus on us now to rekindle our personal and collective relationship with these woodlands, to become familiar with the dappled light of mixed canopies, where oak, ash, alder, birch and hazel intertwine; where delicate wood anemones, dog-violets, bluebells and primroses erupt each spring; where jays screech noisily and ospreys hunt. We have a responsibility to get to know these places, to learn their ways and be nourished by their presence. If we are to have any hope of seeing woodlands protected and expanded, we need to fall back in love with their wild inhabitants.

Looking to the future, our collective appetite for being in wild places will be the power that drives ecological restoration, which in turn has the power to redress many of the environmental problems we face, from the personal to the planetary.

Invitations to the Wild Embrace

🌱 Learn to recognise native trees, beginning with the 'nobles of the wood' under the Brehon Laws: oak, ash, hazel, holly, crab apple, yew and Scots pine.

🌱 Visit the National Museum of Ireland – Archaeology in Kildare Street in Dublin to view stone axes from Neolithic times, ceremonial jewellery from the Bronze Age, and other archaeological artefacts from long ago.

🌱 Try your hand at a traditional craft, such as willow basket weaving or wood carving.

Foraging is
mindfulness
in action

Foraging

ORAGING is innate to us. Humans have always gathered the roots, leaves, stems, fruits and seeds of wild plants to prepare food, medicine, dye and other everyday things. When we gather up wild nettles or rosehips, we are doing exactly what every generation that came before us would have done, right back to the hunter-gatherers who lived here 10,000 years ago.

There are over 200 edible wild plants native to the Irish landscape, ranging from hawthorn leaves to the starchy roots of wild water lilies. There are a great many uses of wild plants in the treatment of ailments, too, as practised by medical herbalists. Willow bark, for example, was a staple of ancient Irish folk medicine. Its value as a remedy was backed up by modern medicine when silicic acid – the anti-inflammatory compound found in willow bark – was synthetically reproduced as aspirin, a staple of modern medicine cabinets.

Today we don't have the same need to forage for wild plants as our ancestors did, but there is much to be said in praise of foraging nonetheless. It is a good reminder that every fruit, vegetable, nut, seed, grain, herb and spice in the world has been bred from wild plants. The flavours of wild-picked fruits and vegetables are often far richer than their cultivated descendants, as flavour is seldom prioritised when selecting varieties for commercial production. Mass-produced cultivars of the original wild ancestor have been bred for size, quantity, uniformity and other pragmatic characteristics. Their foraged counterparts are the real deal, just as nature intended.

A huge part of the attraction of foraging nowadays is the quest to find the thing. This can be great fun, as is the novelty of bringing home your cache to concoct syrups, jams, salads or booze. And of course, nothing compares to the taste of wild strawberries, fraocháns (wild bilberries) and blackberries, which I delight in picking every year. Through foraging, we tune into the seasons. Becoming familiar with even a handful of wild edible plants opens up a whole new adventurous and productive way to engage with nature.

Poking about for wild leaves, fruits or fungi is also an excellent way to slow down, get absorbed in the quest and observe the natural world. Focused like this, our powers of observation sharpen. Foraging is mindfulness in action.

When picking blackberries in August, keep an eye out for silver-washed fritillary butterflies hovering on bramble bushes, their stunning rust-coloured wings opened to the late summer sun. If not for the act of picking wild berries, it's easy to miss these butterflies, thus passing by an opportunity to observe their beautiful wing patterns. Slowing down to eye up fraocháns in a ditch, you might hear the singing of grasshoppers from the field behind. Without stopping to pick a few of these tasty little bilberries, it's easy to stride past without noticing the grasshoppers. In autumn, loading up a basket of rosehips, you might hear the hen harrier's high-pitched call in the distance, a sound we might fail to hear were it not for the slowed pace required for foraging.

Some Easy Food Plants to Forage For

Nettles

Nettles have been prepared and eaten for aeons as a nutritious food and to help cleanse the blood in spring. These super common plants grow abundantly all over the country, especially in rich soils, from which they absorb large amounts of nutrients into their leaves. Full of iron, potassium, calcium and vitamins A, B and C, nettles have been traditionally gathered and cooked in springtime, as a tonic to replenish and energise the body after the long winter. In County Cavan, there is a custom of eating nettles at least three times during Lent. That there are as many as 18 different names for nettle in the Irish language is an indication of how widely utilised they were. In Ulster Irish nettles are known as *cál faiche*, translating as 'field cabbage'. They were even grown under glass in early spring to give the young plants, known as 'early spring kale', a boost. Nettles can provide us with excellent nutrition when not many other green vegetables are available.

When picking nettles, look out for butterflies and caterpillars. Nettles provide good shelter and sustenance for butterflies laying their eggs. Peacock butterflies emerge from hibernation in spring, and after seeking out some flower nectar for energy, lay their little green eggs on the underside of nettle leaves, using a special glue to fix them in place. After a few weeks, the caterpillars hatch out amid a feast of nettles. Small tortoiseshell butterflies also lay their eggs exclusively on nettle leaves, so can be seen fluttering around sunny patches of nettles in spring. Once they hatch, small tortoiseshell caterpillars build a communal nest, like a webbed tent that cloaks the tips of the nettle plant, inside which they can chomp away in relative safety. Listen out for crickets too, as some species, such as the speckled bush cricket, are known to be fond of eating them.

To avail of the goodness of nettles, pick them in March and April, when the sprigs of young leaves growing at the tip of each shoot can be easily plucked from the plant. Gloves will help you avoid being stung. Check for caterpillars and rinse well before cooking. Cooking neutralises the sting, as the formic acid that causes the sting is destroyed by heat. Don't pick them to eat after the start of June as the coarser leaves are bitter and act as a powerful laxative.

My favourite way to eat nettles is in a simple soup made with onions, potatoes, stock and a big bowl of nettle tips. They are also good added to stews in the same way you might use young spinach leaves. Nettle tea, as simple as pouring boiling water over fresh-picked or dried nettles, is surprisingly refreshing.

Dandelion

Humble dandelions are one of the most overlooked of wild Irish foods. We tend to resent their vigour and abundance; we frown if there are too many of them in the garden, even though they offer a welcome splash of yellow cheer. Dandelions are an important source of nectar for butterflies and bees, especially early in spring when there is little else in flower. The English name 'dandelion' comes from the French *dents de lion* – 'teeth of a lion' – because of the jagged edges of the leaves.

Every part of the dandelion plant can be eaten. The chunky, tapering roots have long been used in herbal medicine as a tonic to cleanse the liver. Roasted and ground-up roots make a coffee substitute that was widely brewed during the world wars, when trade routes were interrupted and coffee was in short supply. The flowers are edible too. Young tender leaves can be picked right through the spring and the summer and are rich in minerals. Finely chopped, they make a tangy and nutritious addition to salads, and can be cooked up in the same way you cook baby spinach. Just don't eat too many dandelion leaves – they are a strong diuretic and hence are also known as 'pissy-bed'.

Wild Strawberries

In June, wild strawberries are ripening in hedge banks. Their pea-sized fruits are so intensely strawberry flavoured, they almost taste as though they have been artificially over-enhanced, like strawberry-flavoured jelly sweets. Wild strawberries are best eaten as you find them. The process of watching for them as you stroll slowly along the hedge bank induces a gorgeously immersive state of observation. Even if you have the self-control to gather without gobbling them immediately, they are easily bruised so don't travel well.

Sorrel Leaves

Common sorrel is a small, low-growing leafy plant that is common in grasslands. The little arrow-shaped leaves are surprisingly zesty and a refreshing thirst quencher; a treat to pick and pop straight in the mouth when out and about. I love nibbling on sorrel leaves when on rambles through upland pasture or hilly boreens. They are packed with vitamin C; eating them fresh feels like chomping on a vitamin pill plucked straight from the earth. There is a long tradition in Ireland of using sorrel leaves to make tangy sauces. They are also a great addition to soups and omelettes.

Fraocháns

In July, juicy wild bilberries are ripe, their dark skin peeking out from the leafy little bushes that produce them. I call them fraocháns because that's what they're known as in County Wicklow where I grew up, but they are called whorts in Munster, heather berries in Donegal, bilberries in Connaught and blueberries elsewhere. Fraocháns grow abundantly in acidic and peaty soils, flourishing on mountainsides, in oak woodland, and amid birch and rowan trees.

There is a folk tradition of young people heading up into the hills for 'Fraochán Sunday', which falls on the last Sunday of July. This coincides with the Celtic celebration of Lughnasa, one of the quarterly festivals of the old Celtic year which marked the turning of the seasons, so it is possible that Fraochán Sunday is a continuation of that tradition.

During World War Two, when fruit was in short supply in England, people here headed up to the mountains to pick fraocháns for export. In 1941 alone, Ireland exported 400 tonnes of wild bilberries to England. Foraging earned much-needed cash in tough times.

Picking fraocháns in July is a wonderful way to spend an hour or two, listening to the melodious singing of a skylark hovering in the air above, watching cloud shadows pass over the hills, or catching sight of a hare leaping over heather. Fraocháns seem to have an affinity for beautiful landscapes. They can be eaten fresh, added to porridge or other breakfast dishes, or used in a good old-fashioned fruit crumble. They also freeze well.

Blackberries

Picking and eating blackberries is one of my favourite things to do. Thorny shoots of bramble have a way of establishing themselves wherever there is a gap, growing up and out at an alarming rate, laying down roots wherever they touch the ground. Because of this, brambles and their fruits – blackberries – are abundant everywhere. They erupt behind the fence, down the back of the garden, using their backward-turned thorns to help them hold on as they scramble through hedges and over field corners, even clambering into the woodshed. It's just as well brambles produce such a profusion of blackberries at the end of each summer, sustenance for humans, badgers, foxes, mice, blackbirds, thrushes and many more.

Blackberries are so abundant, sweet and nutritious, it's hardly surprising that they were a major part of our ancient ancestors' diets. Seeds of blackberries have been found by archaeologists in Mesolithic hunter-gatherer sites, and in the centuries before sugar, the annual bounty of blackberries would have been a special treat indeed.

Gather them up in August and September from nearby hedges or wild corners. Eat them fresh. Store them in the freezer to add to breakfast or desert. Infuse them in brandy along with plenty of sugar to make blackberry brandy, ready after about 12 months. And if you ever find yourself stuck for black hair dye, an effective traditional version can be concocted from the roots and leaves of bramble plants.

Wild Carrot Seeds

The tall flower and seed heads of plants in the wild carrot family are shaped like an upside-down umbrella, a structure known as an umbel. In summer the umbel is adorned with hundreds of tiny white flowers. By September, each little flower will have developed into a tiny brown seed. This family of plants is extremely common across Ireland. Several different species in the family are broadly similar in appearance, including hemlock and hogweed, which can be poisonous. Contact with the leaves can cause a burning skin rash, so be sure you know what you are picking, and don't mistake hogweed for wild carrot.

That said, the tiny seeds of wild carrot are well worth learning to recognise for their powerful and surprising taste. I often nibble on them when out and about for a fun blast of unexpectedly strong flavour.

Rosehips

As September begins, bright shiny red rosehips swell from the pollinated core of wild roses, a tangy treat for both birds and mammals. Rosehips are reputed to contain a higher concentration of vitamin C, by weight, than any other wild fruit in this part of the world. For this reason, these shiny red globes have long been harvested in large quantities and made into syrups to boost immunity against winter colds and fever. During World War Two, when citrus fruits became unavailable, hundreds of tonnes of wild rosehips were gathered in government-backed campaigns in the UK and used to make rosehip syrup, in an effort to keep people well dosed up with vitamin C through the war years.

Wild rosehips are easy to find, weaving their way through hedges everywhere. Seeking them out in the tangle of an autumn hedge is a wonderful excuse to linger outdoors, just when trees are treating us to bursts of vivid yellow, rich russet and deep crimson. That rosehips ripen through autumn seems a perfectly synchronous vitamin-rich offering from nature, boosting our immunity as our bodies adjust to winter.

Elder

Elder bushes become laden with big bursts of white flowers in June and with a copious quantity of elderberries in September. Each individual flower is tiny, but they grow all packed together as clusters on elder bushes and trees, wafting out their beautiful scent to call the attention of hoverflies and other pollinating insects. Moths and butterflies suck up the nectar from elderflowers too. Nesting songbirds feed in turn on these insects, spilling the bounty of elder up along the wild food chain.

Elders grow in hedges, woodland edges, abandoned places and often beside old ruins. They blossom during June and are so plentiful that gathering up elderflowers to make cordial, elderflower fizz and elderflower wine is easy wherever you live. Elderflower wine is one of the best country wines. A batch brewed in June will be ready by December, when the sweet smell of elderflowers in the heart of winter casts a gorgeous reminder of long summer evenings.

From August, scraggly little elder trees up and down the country are laden with masses of dark purple berries, gobbled enthusiastically by blackbirds, starlings and thrushes. In one study, more bird species were found to eat elderberries than any other fruit. The birds depend on elder for nourishment, while the elder depends on birds to spread its seed far and wide.

Humans too have been eating elderberries for longer than we know. Elderberries have antiviral properties and are packed with vitamins, so they give a welcome boost to the immune system and can help the body fend off colds and flu as autumn sets in. Elderberry syrup is easy to make and is a tasty addition to porridge or sweet treats.

Hazelnuts

Hazelnuts are supremely nutritious woody pellets of energy that were unsurprisingly gathered and eaten in large quantities by Mesolithic hunter-gatherers and by everyone since.

They have almost as much protein by weight as fish, and can be stored for up to 12 months. Nuts can be picked and eaten from August, when they are still green and fresh-tasting, or harvested in September and October when the nut becomes drier and develops a stronger flavour. There are endless traditional recipes incorporating hazelnuts, for breakfasts, in tea-brack and in crackers. They can also be ground up with herbs to make pesto-like sauces. Hazel grows abundantly all over Ireland, and cultivated varieties, often called cob nuts, are grown commercially to provide hazelnuts for cereals, praline, chocolate-hazelnut spread, and lots of other yummy things.

When out gathering hazelnuts, you have to tune your eyes into the leaves and branches of hazel trees, a meditation in itself. Look out too for signs of squirrels and wood mice in already opened hazel shells strewn about. When a squirrel eats a hazelnut, it cuts the shell right in half, whereas when a wood mouse eats a hazelnut, they use their sharp teeth to gnaw a hole in the hazelnut shell to extract the nut from within, little by little.

Sloeberries

Blackthorn trees are most noticeable in February and March, when masses of delicate white blossoms erupt along hedges and patches of scrub all over the country. By August and September, round shiny blue-black sloeberries are developing in amongst the long, sharp thorns of blackthorn bushes. Sloeberries are the original wild ancestors of all our modern plums, bred over millennia to favour size and sweetness. Wild sloeberries are not at all as sweet as plums; one nibble will make your face pucker up from the intense tartness on the tongue.

Sloeberries have been uncovered in ancient middens (waste heaps) left by Bronze Age farmers and Vikings alike. They were thought to have been used to make an edible fruit 'leather'. First the seeds are removed, then the flesh is mashed up to make a pulp which is spread thinly to dry, concentrating the sugars and easing the bitter taste. Chewy strips of dried fruit leather preserve well and would have provided good sustenance and valuable vitamins throughout the winter months. Gather sloeberries in October to make sloe gin, a tasty treat come Christmas time.

Seaweed

Taking time to explore some seaweed along Atlantic shores is an enjoyably absorbing thing to do, with so many textures, colours and characteristics to observe. Seaweeds come in many strange and intriguing forms, from dark shaggy little bundles to long silky fronds. Learning to identify a few edible seaweeds is a sure way to tune your eyes to the wonderful variety. In scrambling slowly over rocky shores and inlets, the demands of daily life evaporate, soothed by the sound of waves and the colours of changing skies reflected in rock pools and saltwater puddles. Shore birds – poking their long beaks in the sand for lugworms and other treats – are less likely to fly off if you're moving slowly.

Always part of the Irish diet, seaweed is now growing in popularity as 'sea vegetables', a healthy and nutritious food when eaten in small amounts. Seaweed is rich in minerals and trace elements, particularly iodine. Some species are easy to recognise, especially if you're first shown by someone in-the-know. Soon you'll be able to confidently harvest small amounts and save it for use in the kitchen. Most seaweeds can be harvested from spring to autumn.

There is a particular thrill in timing the tides to explore for seaweed, but always make sure to look up tide tables or an app with the tides for that specific location, as tides can turn quickly. Getting caught in an incoming tide can leave you stranded and can be dangerous.

Before you go foraging for seaweed, learn how to harvest sustainably. As with all seaweeds you gather, don't ever pull from the base (called the 'hold fast'), which is where each plant attaches itself to the rock. Only harvest in small amounts. For each piece of seaweed you harvest, don't cut too near the hold fast, just trim a little from the tips, like a gentle haircut, as many seaweeds won't grow back easily from severe harvesting. A good rule of thumb is to trim off no more than a third, always using a sharp scissors or knife.

One of the easiest seaweeds to recognise is dilisk, also known as dulse, which comes in thin sheets of rich wine- to pink- coloured fronds. My father often talked about what a treat it was to have some dilisk to chew on as a child in Belfast in the 1930s, when it was sold from street vendors with hand carts.

Carrageen moss, also known as 'Irish moss', is a small, bushy, purple-coloured seaweed that is traditionally harvested as a type of natural gelatine, used to make puddings with rhubarb or sweet fruits. It is also a renowned traditional cure for coughs, colds and chesty ailments.

Sea spaghetti has long spaghetti-like fronds of olive green growing from a 'button' attached to rock. It grows on the lower shore so is accessible only when the tide is far out. A similar-looking seaweed is called fisherman's line or bootlace weed, which is thinner with un-branched fronds. It is also edible. Only snip a little from some fronds.

One of the most familiar of seaweeds here is bladderwrack, which has been on the secondary school biology curricula for decades as *fucus vesiculosus*. In late summer, bladderwrack develops reproductive tips (not the same as the round 'bladders' that are so characteristic of this seaweed), which are easy to learn to recognise, and happen to be delicious. Trim them off with a scissors and eat them fresh. They taste like salty wild olives.

Serrated wrack is similar-looking bladderwrack, though

does not have the latter's 'bladders'. It is the seaweed traditionally used in seaweed baths, wonderful for the skin.

Always be super careful when out foraging for seaweeds, as seaweeds are algae and are by their nature very slippy. Seaweed harvesting takes a certain skill, and there are lots of things not to do, but it is well worth taking the time to learn a few species and the basics of safe and sustainable harvesting. I highly recommend going on a guided seaweed foraging trip if you are interested in learning about seaweed, as the best way to learn is to be shown. You will get guidance on where to look, how to identify the tastiest species, and how to harvest sustainably.

Before cooking or drying harvested seaweeds, wash them in fresh, clean water to rinse away any little shells or debris. Dry them well if you wish to keep them for use in the kitchen.

Beware of harvesting seaweed in locations where there is a lot of green seaweed, as this could be an indicator that there is a nutrient seepage to the shore, such as sewage or animal slurry, both of which contain harmful bacteria. Seaweed foragers should be advised that a seaweed harvesting licence is required, even if you are harvesting for personal use, and never take from designated nature conservation areas such as a Special Protection Area (SPA) for Birds or a Special Area of Conservation (SAC), where contain rare and highly sensitive species also live.

Mushrooms

Fungi are fascinating, beautiful, daunting, weird and familiar. They grow in grasslands, woodlands, lawns and peaty upland pastures too, emerging from cowpats and tree trunks, fallen leaves and garden sheds.

These intriguing organisms have adapted to grow in almost every ecological niche on the planet, existing in ways that scientists are only beginning to understand. Neither plant nor animal, but a kingdom all of their own, fungi don't have the capacity to photosynthesise; instead they get their energy second-hand like we do. They form incredible symbiotic relationships with plants and animals, which is explored further in the chapter titled 'Symbiosis'.

What we recognise as a mushroom is just the fruiting body of a much larger, unseen organism, existing as filaments that weave their way through the soil or dead wood or whatever substrate the species is adapted to. Some mushrooms are medicinal and some are nutritious. Plenty are edible, though only a few are really worth eating. They come in a colossal array of shapes, sizes and colours, but learning to identify a few of your favourite common edible species will give you an extra reason to make time to get out into woods and fields each autumn.

In Ireland there is often wariness around picking and eating wild mushrooms. Some species are a little poisonous, some can be lethal, some are hallucinogenic, and others are just indigestible so might give you a sore tummy. However, the joy of both picking and eating mushrooms makes acquiring enough knowledge to forage with confidence is well worthwhile. It's not difficult to learn a few species and become familiar with where they grow. In other European countries, including Sweden, Germany, France, Italy and Poland, foraging for wild mushrooms is a widely practised popular pursuit, and autumnal mushroom feasts are commonplace.

If you are curious to learn how to forage for mushrooms, the best way is to go on a mushroom foraging course. Now that there is a welcome surge of interest in mushrooms here, excellent teachers and courses are available all over Ireland through late summer and autumn months.

Common field mushrooms are easy to identify and find. This delicious variety was once widely harvested here. When field mushrooms first emerge in their grassy habitats, they are small white buttons with delicate pink gills. They flatten out as they mature, and the gills turn darker. But even if you think you know them, consult at least one, preferably two proper guidebooks to be sure you know what you are gathering. It's often worth asking older people in your locality too, who will have memories of collecting field mushrooms in summer.

Chanterelles are absolutely delicious and quite common in Ireland, growing in deciduous woodlands from August to December. They are trumpet shaped and bright yellow to orange, like an egg yolk. If you should find a few chanterelles growing, remember the spot, don't tell anyone where it is and return every year.

A Word of Caution about Foraging

All of the wild foods I've described here are abundant, adaptable common species. Nonetheless, when foraging, never take more than a small portion of the leaves or fruits. Leave enough so that the plant can recover easily, and leave plenty for wildlife too. For obvious reasons, do not gather where weedkiller, insecticides or fungicides may have been applied.

Always be sure of the plant you are collecting from, and if in doubt, don't eat it. Ideally go along with someone who knows what they're doing and learn from them. In recent years some excellent foraging courses have been run by knowledgeable and enthusiastic guides. Doing a course can give you the confidence you need to get started on your foraging adventure. There are also some great guidebooks. See the 'Further Reading' section at the end of the book for suggestions.

Invitations to the Wild Embrace

🌱 Harvest nettle tops in spring and make a tasty soup with them. Following an old Cavan tradition, do this three times during Lent for a healthy spring boost of vitamins and minerals.

🌱 Go on a guided seaweed foraging excursion. Time it with a spring tide when much of the intertidal zone is accessible and there will be lots of different seaweeds to examine and identify.

🌱 Collect blackberries at the end of summer and invite friends over to feast on fresh blackberries and ice cream.

🌱 Brew up an immune-boosting rosehip syrup in autumn to keep winter colds at bay.

Being curious
is good for
our brains

Knowing Nature

TODAY, we are at a critical juncture, faced with a narrow window of time to transform our relationship with the natural environment, lest we push remaining ecosystems past the point of collapse. This is an opportunity for each of us to consciously reawaken a loving and nurturing relationship with the natural world, and for each of us to discover for ourselves a wealth of beauty, symbiosis and balance.

When we 'take time to smell the roses', the textures, colours, patterns, scents and sounds around us begin to reveal themselves. These little awakenings can occur during simple everyday routines, such as walking to work or taking a stroll with the dog in the local park. Being out and about in a state of mindful awareness of nature opens us up to rich wonders: the colours in the sky, the sounds of a flock of sparrows in a tree, the pattern of lichen growing on a rock, or the tiny scarlet flowers that blossom from hazel trees in January, so small that you might never see them without looking carefully.

Going out in nature, wherever that might be, without a specific purpose, can be an enlightening experience. In a state of receptiveness, otherwise mundane moments can transform into mesmeric experiences. Allowing for slots of time in nature when we 'do nothing' enhances our creative abilities. Time and space provide fertile soil for the germination of ideas. Simply daydreaming outdoors boosts our problem-solving capacities and opens us up to new perspectives and approaches. Whatever the setting, opening our senses to our surrounds can be surprisingly rewarding.

Each of us can train our minds to be more porous to subtle details. As you move through your environment, simply observe natural textures and movements. By a canal, look out for bulrushes swaying at the edge of the water or colourful damselflies hovering at the water's edge in summertime. As you pass by a hedgerow, you might observe a turquoise caterpillar in a bramble bush, or movement in the leaves that give away the presence of a delicate little chiffchaff or a willow warbler.

We can too easily miss the seductive smell of nectar emanating from an urban wall covered in flowering ivy. Its beautiful, rich scent wafts out from the understated little ivy flowers from September to November, chemical signals travelling all the way from the ivy flower to our nose, a special olfactory treat so late in the year. Ivy flowers produce their enticing scent to advertise to bees and other flying insects that sweet nectar is on offer; it's simply a bonus that we can smell it too.

Everyday experiences such as this can enrich our days, prompting us to pause and breathe deeply, to look up and perhaps get a chance to observe a bumblebee packing pollen into the pouches on its back legs that have evolved especially for this purpose. Imagining the world from alternative perspectives can be fun and enlightening. For example, when you next peer into a tubular foxglove flower, look closely at the polka-dotted pathway inside: a landing strip that invites visiting bees to the source of the nectar at the core of the flower. Then imagine being a bee, landing on the velvety pink cushion of a foxglove flower, completely enveloped in pink light and attention-grabbing patterns. To see a foxglove from the viewpoint of a bee as it ventures in is to empathise with other ways of being.

An animal's perspective may be very different to our own. Many insects see ultraviolet light, which has shorter wavelengths than what our human eyes can detect. Butterflies have patterns on their wings cast in pigment that absorbs ultraviolet light, so what looks like a fairly plain set of blue wings to us, appears as a richly patterned wing to another butterfly.

Flowers, too, whose purpose is to invite in butterflies or other specific pollinators, have patterns in the ultraviolet spectrum on their petals that are invisible to the human eye. These ultraviolet markings make the flower more noticeable and more attractive to insects. Some flowers have a bullseye pattern on their petals which helps orientate the insect towards the centre of the flower, where it will find the nectar while the flower douses its visitor in pollen grains.

Mingling knowledge with imagination allows us to conceive of the world differently. I consider this to be an essential practice for connecting with the wonders of the natural world. It's a good exercise to remind us that our experience of the world is simply that, our experience, and reality is not absolute. With practice, this imaginative process of experiencing the world from other species' perspectives becomes second nature, if you will excuse the pun.

Cultivating Curiosity

A strong body of scientific evidence shows that being curious is good for our brains. Things seen, heard or experienced for the first time trigger the body to produce noradrenaline, a neurotransmitter with hugely beneficial effects on the networks in our brains. According to experts in brain health, curious people live longer because of these effects, and are less likely to become weary, bored or cynical. Even the experience of living in the same neighbourhood, where familiarity can morph into predictability, can be transformed by cultivating curiosity in the details of trees, lichens, birds and other wild organisms around us. As well as being a power workout for the brain, being curious is one of the ways that we can deepen our connection to nature.

Pursuing curiosity leads to endless discoveries about the characters who live alongside us. Robins, blackbirds and other common songbirds, for example, can sing more notes than there are on a standard piano in under one second. Migrating geese arrive back from Greenland in October, passing noisily over city suburbs during winter months, flying in a V-shaped formation so that each goose travels in the slipstream of the one in front. Stunning pyramidal orchids pop up on the bend of the road we cycle each day, adorning summer mornings with their intricately designed pink flowers. Rosehips swell in the forgotten corner behind the shed as summer morphs into autumn, their red pigments signalling to passing animals that they are ready to be eaten. Opening our eyes to these everyday experiences enhances our curiosity as we seek to find out more about what we are seeing, hearing, smelling and touching.

Cultivating curiosity in nature, we realise that the more we learn, the more we want to know. The more we notice and seek out, the more our attention is drawn to question and discover. Noticing the small details and becoming curious to find out more is generally considered a childish trait, but the open, probing wonder of a child is an attitude we can all benefit from nurturing.

Observation as a Source of Knowledge
Practising our skills of observation and enquiry is key to developing the curious mind. We have at our disposal an

unprecedented means of amassing information, whether that's from books, online videos or interest groups in social media. Yet there is nothing to replace a simple walk in nature, where we look out for or discover an intriguing thing, then seek to find some information about that thing.

There is an exercise I often encourage workshop participants to engage in – from youth group leaders to recovering addicts – a fun way to train an enquiring mind and challenge our inhibitions about asking silly questions. If you were a participant in one of these workshops, I would ask you to find something that is 'made by nature' which draws your attention. It could be a feather from a bird, a flower, a lichen-encrusted twig or a butterfly wing. What makes it distinctive? What questions does its physical form raise? What is its function? Asking questions like this will help you to see things from the perspective of the living entity that made that 'thing'.

Why does that plant go to the trouble of creating such geometrically perfect and brightly coloured flowers? What exactly is a lichen? Why do butterflies have such elaborately patterned wings, when a bluebottle can manage just fine with plain little translucent wings?

Asking simple questions like this, from the perspective of the plants or animals that you're observing, can lead you to stumble upon some surprising insights, as it has done for me. Wonder is not just for children; it is for all of us to cultivate. It will sustain our intrigue with nature throughout our lives.

You can cultivate the question-asking process that I describe above as a daily practice. For example, consciously observe the same stretch of river on your regular walks, and notice the seasonal changes of plants, insects, birds and other living things there. You might apply the approach to a tree – ideally a native tree species – by visiting regularly to observe all the things living, growing, feeding and roosting on that tree throughout the seasons.

Make notes, or if you're more of a visual person, draw sketches or take photographs. Where something gives rise to a question, you can later research and in that way enhance your understanding, all the while deepening your relationship with nature.

The more we know of our natural world, the more our wonder is deepened. Take lichens. In Ireland, there are more than a thousand different species of them. Each is a symbiotic partnership between a fungus and an algae. One of the spreading yellow lichens that grows on rocks can live for thousands of years.

Encountering a meadow in high summer full of tall, shimmering yellow field buttercups is a wonderful sight. It's hard not to be moved by their serene beauty. When I investigated what made buttercups shimmer so spectacularly, I was amazed at what I discovered. Buttercup petals are lined with a layer of yellow pigment, which is covered by a super-thin film of minutely engineered air chambers, like bubbles.

These bubbles reflect light back through the yellow pigment, enhancing the intensity of the yellow whilst also creating a far-reaching shimmer.

This impressive physical engineering is how the buttercups attract pollinators from afar, the light acting like a beacon to invite hoverflies and bees to come to rest in the flowers. In addition, the flowers are shaped like satellite dishes, raising the temperature in the centre of the flower by as much as three degrees. This helps to ensure that the insects who land are tempted to linger long enough to pick up plenty of pollen before moving on, hopefully to another shimmering buttercup flower. What a feat of engineering is a simple buttercup flower.

For just over a decade, I have been splitting my time between Dublin and a remote valley in west Cavan. The many hills and hollows in the wide valley have escaped being transformed into high-yielding, fertiliser-doused ryegrass fields – the sad fate of so many Irish townlands since the 1980s. Here, fields are instead packed with wild orchids in spring and summer. As the colour palette of rough pastures changes when summer morphs into autumn, tall golden flower spikes of bog asphodel fill the boggier fields and bouncing purple spheres of devil's-bit scabious abound. Most days I walk to the river along a winding road, wide enough for only one car to pass between the hedges that flank either side. These hedges are here a long time, probably established through a combination of human hand, squirrel-stashed hazelnuts, and seed-bearing bird poo.

The character of the fields changes with every bend in the boreen. I have come to know the route well, familiar with exactly where the wild strawberries grow in June, where the orchids emerge in a profusion of pink pyramids or delicate whites, and where the juiciest blackberries are to be found come August. The opportunity to see the progression of plants and animals throughout the year has allowed me to learn a lot.

Deepening our understanding of the plants and animals we encounter can change our perspective about what we see and how we behave. For me, rather than feeling so sad about the pace and severity of ecological loss that my work brings me to encounter on a regular basis, I now have a relationship with the natural world that is joyful. This helps to counter-balance feelings of overwhelm.

And with cultivating knowledge comes the ascribing of value. As humans, we have no difficulty celebrating man-made feats of artistry and engineering, while our collective ego blinds us to the incredible feats of artistry and engineering that nature produces. These are often complex beyond anything imaginable by the human mind, awesome beyond description – whether it be the suction of a limpet, bound to a rock by the strongest substance known to humankind (now being copied for use in spacecraft), or the agility of a kingfisher that can dart from a branch to catch a fish and be back on its branch within 1.2 seconds.

Learning to value the everyday wonders of nature can

motivate us to engage with the complex environmental challenges of our time, inspiring action from a more centred and connected place.

Invitations to the Wild Embrace

❦ Spend time in the outdoors doing nothing in particular, allowing yourself to passively watch movements, gradients of colour and textures.

❦ Tune into the sounds of nature.

❦ Being still, take time to examine the patterning of veins on a leaf, the geometry of moss, or the arrangement of branches on a tree.

❦ Find something 'made by nature' which appeals to you. Observe its structure closely and allow as many questions as you can to arise. If your chosen object is a bird feather, for example, ask yourself why the shaft is hollow and why it might be coloured as it is. If it's a seashell, examine the patterns and see what you can figure out about the creature that made it.

Irish names can
be evocative,
insightful and fun

What's in a Name?

MY journey learning the names of plants and animals began when I was in my late teens. I bought a 'flora' – a guidebook with a key to the identification of wild plants – and looked up many of the plants I encountered on my forays through hills, woodlands and sand dunes. I kept a little notebook and recorded what I learnt, making a note of the plant's characteristics that jumped out at me, the name, time of year, where I had seen it, and what it looked like to me.

I would sometimes make up names for particular plants when I couldn't figure out their actual names. I would continue my understanding of the plant by the name I had given it, learning where it grows and what it looks like, eventually switching to its 'real' name when I managed to identify it. This is the reason why I still call 'selfheal' my own made-up name of 'Japanese towers', after the way that its pyramidal stack of purple flowers is so architecturally arranged. It's a name I made up 20 years ago, and I still struggle to remember selfheal's 'real' name. Learning can be fun, and we don't always need to confine or categorise what we see according to the accepted botanical nomenclature.

Keeping a notebook is really helpful for learning about wildlife. I still go through new notebooks regularly, and love looking back over old notebooks from my late teens and twenties. It's also nice in winter to glance over your notes from the previous spring and summer and take the time to learn about new plants, trees, birds or damselflies you've seen during the year. Making little sketches and diagrams can be fun, even if, like me, you're not much good a t drawing.

Being able to identify and name a bird, a butterfly or a wildflower is a prerequisite to further research about that species, allowing us to store and file all that we learn about them in our heads under one linguistic tab. Learning to identify various species helps us to remember what they look like, where we saw them before, and what their key characteristics are. It is how we build up our knowledge, learn associations and enhance what we observe when we next encounter that thing. Names give meaning and context.

Knowing the names of plants and animals is how we learn about their preferences: wet or dry, shaded or open, marine or freshwater. We get to read about where they live, who they like to live with, what they eat, how they behave, and their community of associates and competitors (otherwise known as a habitat). Knowing a name is also necessary if we want to find out more about the history, ecology, folklore and uses of that plant or animal.

Think of how tricky it is to gossip about people or celebrities without knowing their names. The same applies to wildlife. Being able to chat with friends and family about our wild encounters is made all the better when we can talk about the things we've seen by using their names. This is the basis for conversations and shared learnings and allows us to share our wonder at seeing the startling blue on the wings of a jay that flew by in the woods that morning, or recount the soundtrack of the grasshoppers singing as we strolled past the meadow with a friend.

Reclaiming Relevance

There is also a deeper relevance to learning the names of wildflowers, berries, trees, birds, butterflies and damselflies. In just a generation or two, we have been cleaved apart from our roots in nature, more attuned now to marketing slogans than elements of our environment. Losing our knowledge of the names of things is a symptom of our growing separation from nature, creating a vacuum that gets filled instead with knowledge of brand names and consumer goods. In an age where children and adults alike can identify dozens of logos, few can identify ten native trees. Advertising jingles are more familiar than the songs of common birds.

In 2007, the *Oxford Junior Dictionary* purged a number of words that had previously been included, including acorn, bluebell, buttercup, catkin, fern, hazel, nectar, pasture and willow. Their reasoning was that these words are no longer in common use, and the dictionary needed to make room for new words such as blog, broadband, chatroom and voicemail. The removal of everyday words relating to nature from such a dictionary reflects how words such as 'nectar' and 'acorn' are falling out of regular use, even falling into obscurity. When we drop these words from the language we use, we abandon their relevance in our lives; we 'cancel' them from our culture.

Using words that describe the natural world reinstates their relevance. Learning the names of things is core to the process of re-entangling ourselves with wild things. The deeper significance of learning the words for plants and animals is that words in any language carry cultural significance.

The words we use frame our perception. Across the world, the loss of indigenous languages is deeply entwined with the loss of biodiversity. To the ancient Irish-speaking inhabitants of Ireland, the land, soil, plants, trees and rivers were all suffused with meaning, sometimes utilitarian, sometimes spiritual. For millennia, people had complex and intimate connections with every component of the living world. These connections were as diverse as the species and habitats that sustained them. It is often the case that the names of plants and animals have arisen from daily interactions or meanings associated with that plant or animal. Becoming familiar with names and some of the traditional uses of wild plants is one way of reviving these deep-rooted connections.

Common and Scientific Names

Most fungi, plants and animals have a common name, perhaps a local or colloquial name, and a scientific (or binomial) name, which draws heavily on Greek or Latin. Common names can be evocative, or tell us something about the thing; for example, plants with 'wort' in their name were often used medicinally: toothwort would have been traditionally used for easing toothache, woundwort for treating wounds, and pilewort for treating piles.

Scientific names can tell us about the characteristics of the plant or animal, or its habitat. *Officinalis* means that it was used medicinally. When *palustre* is used in the name, it means that it is happy in wet places. *Vulgaris* means common; for example, the scientific name for common selfheal (the 'Japanese towers' mentioned above) is *Prunella vulgaris. Alba* means white, which could refer to the back of leaves (as with *Salix alba* – white willow), or to a plant with white flowers, such as white-water lily (*Nymphaea alba*). When *sylvatic* appears in the scientific name, it suggests that the plant or animal has a woodland association, for example *Luzula sylvatica*, the 'greater wood rush'. *Odorata*, meaning perfumed, is used in the name for *Viola odorata* – the sweetly perfumed wood violet. Unsurprisingly, *maritima* means coastal, used for plants such as sea thrift, which grows in bunches of lovely purple spheres often seen on coastal rocks; their scientific name is *Armeria maritima*.

Learning the scientific names for species is not for everyone, though it can be illuminating and interesting to those with an appetite for language.

Irish Names

I also like to learn the Irish names for wild plants and animals. Often, the Irish names are both evocative and insightful. The kingfisher's Irish name is *cruidín* or *cruitín*, the Irish word for a hunchback, evoking the hunched-over look that kingfishers have when perched on a branch by the river, watching down intently for a fish to grab and gobble.

Jays are another stunning bird, with pink bellies and a flash of blue wing stripes, though in the clutter of a woodland, jays are seldom seen; instead we know they are about because of their loud, raucous squawk, giving them the Irish name *scréachóg choille* – the woodland screecher.

Sometimes discovering species' Irish names can lead to fun revelations. Certain orchids growing in Kerry are called *magairlín* in Irish, named for their root tubers which are dual bulbous nodes. (*Magairlín* is the word for testicles in Irish.) Because of this resemblance, orchid tubers were used in west Kerry as a love potion. Other Irish words have filtered into everyday use, such as *feileastram*, the Irish name for yellow flag iris, a majestic tall plant that is a kind of a wild lily, filling up wet field corners in summertime.

Cat crainn means 'tree cat' and is the Irish word for pine marten. Roughly the same size as a domestic cat, pine martens are also predators, though they live up in the canopies of trees. *Madra uisce* is the Irish for otter, meaning 'dog of the water'. Some Irish names are funny, such as the word for jellyfish – *smugairle róin* – which translates as seal snot. Sea anemones, as seen in rock pools, can have their tendrils in or out. When in, they look like shapely squidgy blobs, so their Irish name is *cíoch charraige* – which directly translates as rock boob.

Many placenames in Ireland are based on the ecology of that place, incorporating Irish names of trees, habitats or animals.[12] For example, *maigh eo* means the 'plain of the yew' – *eo* being the word for yew. I love to think of County Mayo as a vast expanse of yew trees, a history carried down to us through the original placename.

There are multiple placenames in Ireland containing *broc*, the Irish name for badger, for example, *Domhnach Broc* or Donnybrook in Dublin; and many placenames containing the word *giorria*, which means hare. *Meenagarragh* in Donegal, for example, means the smooth fields of the hare.

Another of my favourite examples is *iolar*, the Irish word for eagle. Before eagles were persecuted to extinction in the nineteenth century, they had been widespread across Ireland.

Ecologists considering their reintroduction here studied the placenames containing *iolar* as a way of estimating the extent of eagle populations in the past. Their research informed the conclusion that well over a thousand pairs of sea eagles and a thousand pairs of golden eagles were resident in Ireland in pre-medieval times. Both golden eagles and white-tailed sea eagles have been re-introduced to Ireland and are now breeding here for the first time in a hundred years.

Invitations to the Wild Embrace

🌱 Find out the Irish name for the townland or parish where you live. Explore its original meaning and what that reveals about the place. The townland where I live, for example, contains the word *beith* which is the Irish for birch tree. Birch trees still grow well in the peaty soils here.

🌱 Whenever you see plants or animals that are new to you, do your best to identify them with a flora or a relevant identification book or app. Make a record of their names and where you first saw them.

🌱 Explore the Irish names of your favourite birds, mammals and other wild creatures – these are often evocative, insightful or fun.

🌱 You could try to learn just one new plant, tree and bird each week and keep records in your notebook. You'll be surprised how much fluency with the natural world this gives you in just one season.

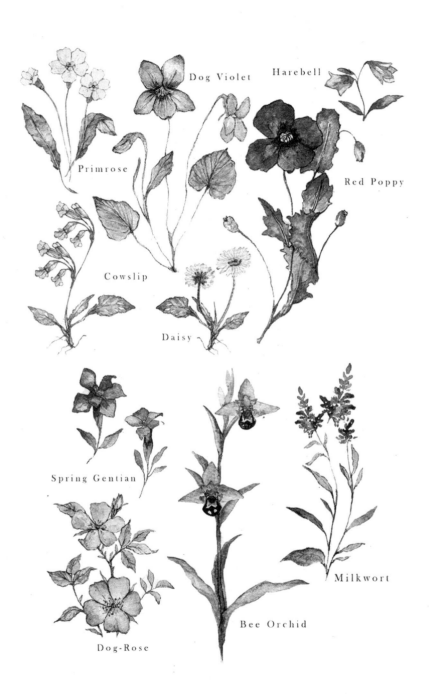

Dog Violet

Harebell

Primrose

Red Poppy

Cowslip

Daisy

Spring Gentian

Bee Orchid

Milkwort

Dog-Rose

Thank
goodness for
plant sex

The Joy of Flowers

P LANTS are the basis of every food chain and the foundation of every ecosystem. Aside from being pretty, flowering plants are one of the most essential components of life on earth. They are also a good 'gateway drug' for greater familiarity with everyday nature.

Flowers are generally the showiest part of the plant, an intricate lure for sexual reproduction. Apart from being colourful, pleasingly symmetrical, and often beautifully patterned, flowers have another great advantage for us: they don't hide themselves, fly away or scuttle off. Their job is to be noticeable. Because plants tend to stay rooted in the same place, their reproductive parts need to stand out so that bees and other pollinating insects know that visits will be well-rewarded with nourishing nectar and pollen.

Far from being frivolous, flowers are how most plants multiply and perpetuate the existence of their kind. Whether a common and often overlooked daisy or a rare and structurally complex orchid, all flowering plants invest a great deal of energy in producing colourful and carefully designed flowers.

Plant Sex

I still find that understanding the basics of plant biology and recognising the essential features of flower structures augments how much I see when admiring a flower. There is so much detail to look for. Plants with showy flowers, such as dandelions, honeysuckle and wild roses, tend to be pollinated by animals, mostly insects. Grasses and other plants with subtle flowering parts usually rely on the wind to disperse their pollen, which negates the need for visual appeal. Because releasing pollen on the wind is not a targeted approach to getting your pollen to another of your kind, these plants have to produce an awful lot more pollen to overcome the odds of such random dispersal.

Some plants go both ways, hedging their bets between the wind and insects, such as our native willow trees. Plenty of plants don't produce flowers at all, including conifer trees, mosses, liverworts, ferns, horsetails, seaweeds and other algae. These plants have other ways of mixing their genes between individuals, such as cones and spores.

Either way, a flower's *raison d'être* is to get the male pollen to the female parts of a flower on a different plant of the same species. Colour is one of the main ways to get noticed by pollinators, but scent can be an important signal too, carefully honed to attract the right pollinator species.

Wandering along a hedge at dusk during late summer, I am sometimes stopped in my tracks by richly perfumed molecules wafting out from honeysuckle flowers. This is a plant that has co-evolved with moths, emitting its sweet scent more intensely at dusk to announce itself to the night-flying moths who pollinate it. Moths have an especially long proboscis, perfectly matched to probe deep inside the long tubular petals of honeysuckle where the nectar is. Honeysuckle flowers are the colour of peaches and cream, which stands out well in the darkness, easier for moths to notice. Bats also come out at dusk and eat a lot of moths, making honeysuckle a draw for them too. For this reason, when you next breathe in the sweet musky smell of honeysuckle flowers at dusk, look out for bats flying overhead.

On a morning walk, keep a nose for hawthorn blossom that actively wafts out its rich aromas. Hawthorn flowers emit their scent most strongly from 7a.m. until 5p.m. each day, the hours during which flies and the bees who gather up the hawthorn pollen are most active. Once each hawthorn flower is pollinated, the pollen-laden anthers change from pink to brown, a transition worth looking out for as May progresses.

Once the pollinator is lured in, it is guided to the nectary – the gland that secretes nectar at the core of the flower. While the bee, moth, butterfly or fly is sucking up their fill of sweet nectar, pollen-bearing anthers positioned just above the nectary release their minute parcels of genetic coding onto the body of insects, who then unwittingly transport these off to another flower. When they get there, the stigma and style (the female parts of the flower) are carefully designed to swipe the microscopic grains of pollen from the body of the visitor. Some flowers contain both male and female organs; others produce flowers with either male or female parts; ideally, there will be an exchange between flowers from separate plants.

Flowers produce astronomical quantities of pollen, though each grain is infinitesimally minute. Pollen grains are as distinctive to the plant that produces them as a flower is, geometrically precise and identifiable. Nettle pollen is shaped like a rugby ball; oxeye daisy pollen like a sea urchin; and water-lily pollen like a donut. A hand lens – a small magnifying lens – allows you to peer into the flower and see the structure of the pollen-bearing stamens, though the pollen grains themselves are often too small to be seen, even with a hand lens.

Once a flower is fertilised, petals are no longer needed. The ovule within starts to swell as the seed develops. Seeds are often rich in protein and fat, making them appealing food for animals. The seed pods of primrose and wild violet, for example, are tasty treats for wood mice. By the time some of the undigested seeds come out the other end of the mouse, he or she will likely have scampered along the hedge or around the other side of the hill, depositing potential new violet and primrose plants with a dollop of nutrient-rich manure to help get the baby plant established.

Sometimes seeds are encased inside a tasty fruit in order to entice an animal to eat them, like blackberries, rosehips, haws and holly berries, though many plants don't bother producing fruits, instead adorning their seeds with appendages to catch the wind. Ash keys have wings and swirl like little helicopters. Tiny dandelion seeds each have their own feathery parachutes to carry them off on the slightest breeze. The familiar white fluffy heads of bog cotton are made up of tiny hairs, each attached to a tiny seed – the plant's mechanism to send its seed off on the wind and colonise new ground.

Some plants have engineered themselves mechanisms to hitchhike on the fur of passing mammals. Cleavers, otherwise known as sticky-backs, grow in parks, gardens and hedges, familiar to many as the tall, sticky stems that you can attach to other people's clothes for fun. Tiny hooks all along its leaves and seeds mean that seeds often travel far in the fur of a fox or a human trouser leg.

Burdock, a common plant that grows alongside hedges and in rough ground, has big barbed seed heads adorned with minute hooks that the plant has engineered specially to attach to the fur of a passing animal. These are the burrs which you will likely have picked from your socks or your dog at some stage, meaning that either you, your socks or your dog have been tricked into being a vector for burdock seeds. These seeds, incidentally, were the inspiration for the invention of velcro.

As with how they spread their pollen, plants have infinite, ingenious ways of spreading their seeds. Both animal pollination and animal-assisted seed dispersal are processes honed over millions of years of evolution. Often, both species benefit from the exchange. Thank goodness for plant sex, for without it, the world would be barren of either flowers or seeds.

Timing

Insects who directly eat living plants have evolved in tandem with the plants, synchronising their life cycles with the growth or flowering phases of their particular food plant. Take cuckoo flowers and orange-tip butterflies, for example. The delicate pale pink blossom of cuckoo flowers (also known as lady's smock) can be seen above the green palette of wet meadows, roadside verges and other damp, flowery habitats during April and May. It is the preferred nectar source of the eye-catching orange-tip butterfly, which can be seen drinking from it just as the flower is blossoming. And because caterpillars of orange-tip butterflies are especially adapted to eat leaves of the cuckoo plant, females lay their eggs on them. Aeons of evolution have honed the life cycles of cuckoo flowers and orange-tip butterflies to become entangled and interdependent, the flower feeding the butterfly, the butterfly carrying the pollen from one cuckoo flower to another, rarely wasting pollen by visiting a different species.

This is an everyday example of two species fulfilling each

other's needs in balanced reciprocity. The plant is the leader of this design plan, producing nectar for the assurance of a reliable and targeted means of transport for its precious pollen. Incidentally, the cuckoo flower gets its name because it flowers when the cuckoo arrives back to Ireland from its African migration, returning to the damp fields and meadows where the cuckoo flower blooms.

Geometry

Flowers often display perfect geometry, with their various parts arranged in accordance with precise mathematical formulae that make them perfectly symmetrical. Genetic coding, like computer algorithms, sets out the precise mathematical formula that leaves, flowers, ovules, tiny grains of pollen and subsequent seeds all conform to.

Cheerful oxeye daisies, for example, which look like daisies on steroids, are an everyday example of perfect geometry. These gorgeous wildflowers erupt on roadside verges and forgotten corners, with a yellow core made up of tightly packed tiny flowers arranged in a spiral symmetry, surrounded by perfectly spaced white petals. The delicate little pink flowers of herb Robert, a common plant of gardens and hedges, display a lovely five-fold geometry, with each purple petal laid out in a precise five-pointed form.

Examining the geometry in flowers is fascinating, a regular reminder that mathematics is the language of nature.

Leonardo da Vinci (1452–1519) made detailed diagrams of the anatomical arrangements of flowers, including the pentagonal geometry of the five-petalled violet. One hundred years later, Galileo, often described as the father of modern science, was an early proponent of exploring the mathematical patterns behind natural phenomena. In 1623 he wrote: 'The grand book of the universe was written in the language of mathematics and its characters are triangles, circles and other geometric figures, without which it is impossible to understand a word of it.' He was a keen observer of the patterns in nature, from the movement of celestial bodies to the geometry of flowers.

Close observation of the symmetry and geometry of flowers is a wonderful meditation on the mathematics of the universe, from the minute to the cosmic.

Thanks, Plants

In the beginning, before plants, the earth's atmosphere contained only tiny quantities of oxygen. It was plants that discovered how to harness the sun's energy, producing carbon-based food for themselves and releasing oxygen as a by-product. This oxygen, made entirely by plants, is what courses through our blood, essential for the functioning of every component of our bodies.

All around us, every minute of every day, tiny green chloroplasts contained in the cells of green plants absorb the energy of photons of light that have travelled here all the way from the sun. The photons excite electrons within the chlorophyll, breaking up molecules of water into hydrogen and oxygen, triggering a tiny but magical reaction that is the basis for all life on earth. The oxygen is released into the atmosphere, making the planet habitable for mammals such as ourselves, and the hydrogen is used to break down carbon dioxide into compounds that are the basis of every food chain on earth. Green plants produce all the energy that sustains every other living being.

And yet our attitude towards plants, generally speaking, is to strim, mow, spray and otherwise control them, or at best abstract them from their natural habitats to grow them in ways that serve our aesthetic or nutritional needs. We cultivate highly modified versions of wild plants as neat rows of crops that provide us with food, fuel and fibre. We plant single species of trees in lines that we call forests, a far cry from diverse, complex and resilient woodland ecosystems.

I like to give plants the appreciation and respect they deserve for figuring out how to make such a wonderful world, for providing us with the oxygen we inhale with every breath and the energy we consume in every bite of food we eat. To hold plants in the high esteem that they deserve, it's good to be able to recognise at least some of the wild plants we come into contact with on a regular basis, learning their names and a little bit about their life strategies.

Observing Plants

When walking with the mind turned inwards, thinking about all things to be done that day, we tend not to take in the incredible detail of the world around us. Marching along at pace, perhaps completing a set distance within a set time, sometimes while listening to a podcast or chatting on the phone with a friend, we miss so much. There is a world of difference between this and walking in nature with our mind tuned to observation mode, taking in the textures and colours of all the things growing along our route, along with the sounds, smells and changing light.

I am often baffled at how many previously unseen details I notice each time I walk with my mind turned outwards. There might be ivy berries ripening in late winter, or masses of creeping vetch, a wild ancestor of peas, in places I hadn't seen them before. I recently looked closely at a beautiful globe of devil's-bit scabious (a tall purple flower that appears in August and September) and noticed a striking turquoise caterpillar on it. I peered closely at another flower nearby and was surprised to see a tiny grasshopper there.

Wildflower Guidebooks

To discover the world of wild plants, it's helpful to have a few tools. A well-annotated flora, or guidebook to wildflowers, is a must for anyone keen to get serious about the identification of wild plants. There are smartphone apps available that can help to identify plants, although these won't push you to train your skills of observation. There is joy in looking at the details of plants: counting petals, observing how the leaves join the stalk, and examining the underside of leaves to see if they are downy or smooth. Using an app can be handy, when they are accurate (they are often not) but try not to use the app in lieu of actually observing the plant.

There are many field guides to wild plants in Britain and Ireland. A book with a 'key' to wildflowers takes you through the steps of identifying plants. Each time you answer yes or no to a question about leaf shape, the number of petals, and so on, the key brings you closer to identifying the family to which the plant belongs, and thus eventually to identify the species of plant. Most flora have drawings and diagrams which are really helpful when observing details and trying to decipher one species from another.

Some wildflower guides are organised according to the colour of the flowers, which can make things easier, especially for the beginner. There are also several excellent books about wildflowers in Ireland which rely on photos. I've included recommendations in the 'Further Reading' section at the end of this book.

Using a Hand Lens

It can be fun to use a hand lens to peer into flowers, and also to look at the fine details of leaves, lichens, mosses and butterfly wings. An old magnifying glass will do just as well, but a hand lens is compact, sturdy and easier to bring around with you. With a hand lens, you can see the detail of the patterns on the petals, the arrangement of pollen on the anthers, and the structure of the stem. The reveal under a hand lens can alter our perspective on scale and beauty.

Invitations to the Wild Embrace

🌱 Learn the names of the most conspicuous, common blooms in your local area.

🌱 Use a magnifying glass or a hand lens (if you can't find one in the shops, you can easily buy one online) to observe the pollen-laden anthers inside a flower.

🌱 Practise 'no-mow May' or, better still, avoid mowing until the end of the summer and prepare to be surprised by the wildflowers that will appear.

🌱 Seek out wild orchids in summertime. There are many types, and some are very rare, though pyramidal orchids are not uncommon and can be found growing on hedge banks, roadside verges and sand dunes.

🌱 Examine the geometry of some common wildflowers such as the five-fold geometry of herb Robert, a common flower of gardens and hedges, or the spiral symmetry at the core of oxeye daisies.

Hedgerows are
the green veins of
the countryside

Hedgerows

MY earliest memory of being in nature is lying underneath a hedge in awe at the blanket of primroses spreading about me. I remember feeling as though I had discovered a treasure, hidden away in a world of shady undergrowth where people didn't tend to venture. I was probably only three or four years old, small enough to clamber easily in underneath the big old hedge. As an adult, I still find the soft yellow perfection of swathes of primroses a magical and reassuring sight.

Ireland's hedgerow habitats are home to lots of wildlife that need the shelter of their shrubby layers. Hedgerows are the green veins of the countryside, through which a wealth of wild animals flow. Here bees find pollen and nectar; little shrews sniff their way about and bats weave above, while kestrels and owls utilise hedgerows to extend their reach through farmland habitats. On a landscape level, hedges act as corridors for the movement and dispersal of wild things. They also give the welcome impression that Irish landscapes are more wooded than they really are.

In winter, the silhouettes of leafless hedgerow trees cast long shadows on sunny days. In spring, the eruption of confetti-like blackthorn blossom is one of the first to brighten the landscape. At the start of summer, whitethorn offers up its bounty of bright flowers to bees and butterflies, while the thicket of thorny trees and bushes offers refuge for nesting birds. In autumn, ash keys, sloeberries, haws and rosehips offer vitamin-rich nutrition to keep both birds and mammals going through the winter months.

Even though hedges are not strictly a 'natural' feature, they are home to an impressive suite of species who make their lives in and around them. Colourful beetles clamber through every level. Solitary bees find suitable nesting holes in the earthen banks of big old hedges. As many as two thirds of Ireland's resident songbirds nest in hedges, finding safety in the thick lower section, where the tangle of whitethorn and bramble offers nestlings the best protection from predatory crows, kestrels and foxes.

Growing caterpillars feed off tree leaves and in turn provide juicy protein-rich meals for baby birds. Wood mice, hedgehogs, barn owls and bats emerge after dusk to hunt for small mammals along the shelter of a good hedge. Foxes, hedgehogs, wrens, robins, blackbirds, painted lady caterpillars and hundreds of other species who live in and around our hedges don't seem to be too fussy about whether their habitat is natural or man-made.

A good thick hedge has most of the features of a woodland edge habitat, where it's neither too shady nor too bright. These are ideal conditions for many fruiting trees, and an excellent surrogate habitat for plants and animals who would otherwise live along a woodland edge.

Hedgerow History

Often the oldest hedges are richest. Medieval hedgerows were constructed to demarcate townland boundaries, when townlands became the fundamental unit of land tenure.[13] Today these townland boundary hedges are recognisable by their extra large earthen banks and the presence of small trees such as hazel, guelder-rose, spindle and crab apple. Generally speaking, the older the hedge, the greater the variety of species it will contain, accumulating arrivals with time.

The majority of Ireland's hedges were planted as recently as the eighteenth century, prompted by a series of 'enclosure acts'. In a time of agricultural 'revolution', open pasture and common land were being parcelled into distinct fields, representing a shift in ownership patterns and facilitating more targeted techniques of animal breeding and crop rotation. Before the days of barbed wire, hedges as living fences made economic sense and had many benefits for the farm. Not only do they keep the cows out of the corn field, but they also offer shelter for farm animals. On a stormy spring day or a baking hot summer afternoon, cows and sheep are generally to be seen gathering near the hedges. I always feel especially sorry for farm animals in fields without hedges to shelter by.

Surrogate Habitat

As many as 50 different plant species can be found growing in just a 3-metre stretch of hedgerow, including trees, shrubs, climbers, small flowering plants, grasses, sedges, ferns, mosses, liverworts and lichens.[14] Each of these provides sustenance for phytophagous invertebrates (insects who eat green plants) such as caterpillars, aphids, beetles, shield bugs and more. In the summer months, look out for red soldier beetles on the flowers of hogweed, often one beetle straddling another as they mate in the umbel of tiny white flowers. A tall crown of hogweed will also feed gazillions of tiny flying insects who suck the sap from stems and eat the nectar of the flowers. These tiny insects are eaten by ladybirds and other hungry beetles, who in turn are fodder for hungry little wrens and blackcaps.

Wrens are one of the more distinctive of hedgerow inhabitants. Their tiny round brown bodies are easy to recognise because of their characteristic upturned tail feathers. As Ireland's second-smallest bird, wrens can certainly make themselves heard from their hideouts in the undergrowth. Males make three or four nests in spring, giving potential partners a choice of which nest she likes best. The male then adds the finishing touches, a lining of soft downy feathers for his mate to lay a clutch of eggs in. Male wrens are serial monogamists, choosing up to three consecutive mates each nesting season. By the time September arrives, a male wren may have built as many as 12 nests that year.

Hawthorn trees form the bulk of most hedges in Ireland. Hawthorn is also widely referred to as whitethorn and as the May-bush, on account of its explosion of white flowers in May. Its Irish name, *sceach gheal*, translates as 'bright thorn'.

Young hawthorn leaves are edible; traditionally they were called 'bread and butter' and were grazed upon by children on their way to school. Lots of animals eat hawthorn leaves too. Lambs love nibbling on them, as do dozens of different caterpillars from both moths and butterflies. The hawthorn shield bug has evolved special brown and green colouring to camouflage itself perfectly against hawthorn leaves.

Hedges are great habitats for climbing plants such as bramble, wild rose and honeysuckle, experts at availing of the support of woody trees and shrubs like holly, hawthorn, blackthorn, hazel and willow. Bramble has an amazing ability to move, for a plant. The tip of each stem waves in slow motion from side to side as it reaches out in search of things to hook itself onto, growing as much as 5 centimetres per day. A tangle of bramble is great protection for young trees, its backward-pointing barbs deterring grazers who might nibble the tree bark. Luckily, bramble is also a wonderful species for wildlife, its generous flowers offering nectar and pollen for bees, butterflies and hoverflies; while its blackberries are a sweet feast for birds, badgers, foxes and field mice.

Most of Ireland's ten different species of native wild rose are happy weaving their way through hedgerow habitats, including dusty pink dog-rose, three species of super-scented wild downy rose, and sweetbriars, whose leaves and fruits smell of apples.

Wild roses are the ancestors of the hundreds of varieties of cultivated garden roses that now exist, though native wild roses are much better for wildlife. The cultivated roses that we grow in our gardens are bred to such an extreme that they no longer contain accessible nectar or pollen for wild bees and butterflies; whereas the open flowers of wild roses allow bees and other pollinating insects easy access to the protein-rich pollen grains and sweet nectar too.

Wild rose leaves are home to several specially adapted tiny creatures, such as the caterpillars who build themselves a protective shelter by sawing a circle out of a wild rose leaf, folding it over and fixing it in place with a sticky string that the caterpillars make themselves. This allows them to chomp away at the leaf beneath without fear of being eaten by a hungry wren or robin.

For a budding plant enthusiast, hedgerow plant communities are one of the easiest to explore. Apart from all the tree species and the climbing plants, a hedge with a decent bank or verge will likely contain a good variety of small flowering plants too. Delicate little dog-violets blossom in spring, their bright blue flowers a gorgeous colour combination alongside yellow primroses. Violets are a great source of nectar for early-emerging butterflies as well as the larval food plant for fritillary butterflies.

One of the most worthwhile hedgerow plants to get to know is wild strawberry. Its cute little white flowers appear on hedge banks in May, five petals precisely placed around a cheerful yellow core. By June, each flower that has been successfully pollinated develops into a delicious little wild strawberry. I always look forward to June, for all the wild strawberries bursting with flavour and sweetness, waiting for me to savour as I walk my regular route to the river near my home.

Wild peas often grow along hedge banks, using their little green curly tendrils to clamber up over taller, sturdier plants, just like the cultivated varieties of pea that are more familiar from the garden. Bush vetch is one species of wild pea whose pretty purple flowers are followed by pods of tiny wild peas. These wild peas are the ancestors of both the sweet peas we grow for their flowers and the peas we eat for dinner. Peas and vetches are nitrogen-fixing plants, transforming atmospheric nitrogen into bio-available nutrients, one of nature's best offerings of plant-based protein.

In May and June, stunning early purple orchids flower. Their eye-catching deep pink flower clusters are beautiful in both colour and form, definitely worth examining through a hand lens for the intricate structure of the flowers and their patterned petals. Pyramidal orchid is another species of wild orchid that grows on hedge banks, roadside verges and sand dunes. Its flower clusters are noticeably pyramidal when they first emerge, filling out into tall cylinders of tightly packed flowers. The striking shape of their flowers attracts the butterflies and moths who pollinate them, reaching with their proboscises into the hearts of the flowers where the nectar awaits.

After midsummer, meadowsweet emerges from roadside verges where the ground is damp. Meadowsweet has tall sprays of many tiny flowers that look like wedding lace. They start out as the most delicate little white pinheads before their petals unfurl. Meadowsweet is recognisable by its strong sweet scent, making it a traditional flavouring for homemade beer.

With so many wild species finding refuge in healthy hedges, some of the top predators are present too. Barn owls emerge at nighttime, hunting along the verges between hedges and fields. An abundance of wood mice, pygmy shrews and small birds sustain majestic kestrels and powerful sparrowhawks.

Whenever you next get a chance, stroll slowly along a decent hedgerow in summertime. Poke about, look for different leaves and flowers, and hunker down to see what's growing underneath. Not every hedge has all the features I describe. The majority of hedges in Ireland are either over-managed, abandoned altogether, or suffering from sheep trampling through the base, but a good thick hedge with a flower-rich verge will be full of life. When you take the time to look closely, a hedgerow habitat will be sure to reveal some of its secrets.

Autumn Fruits

While wild strawberries are ripe in June, and wild blueberries in July, it is at the end of August and during September that hedgerows offer up their most generous bounty. It has taken since spring for the wild roses, brambles, hawthorn and blackthorn to complete their reproductive cycles, harvesting the sun's energy through the summer months, culminating in an abundance of ripe autumn fruits.

This plethora of hedgerow fruits is eagerly gobbled up by birds, wood mice, pine martens, hedgehogs, badgers and foxes. Fieldfares and waxwings are two types of bird who come to Ireland each autumn especially for the abundance of wild autumn fruits in hedgerows here. Fieldfares are particularly keen on rowan berries, whose big bunches of bright red and orange berries stand out beautifully against gently yellowing autumn leaves.

Hawthorn trees produce copious quantities of haws, each the swollen ovule of a successfully pollinated hawthorn flower.

The generous white blossom on blackthorn trees, appearing well before spring equinox, has developed into blackish-blue sloeberries by the time the autumn equinox comes around.

Bright pink, star-shaped spindle berries are one of my favourite hedgerow finds. They are not edible by humans, but the bright orange seeds inside the candy-pink fruits are a gorgeous colour combination.

Hedgerow Conservation and Management

The thing to remember about hedges is that the hawthorn and other trees who provide the framework for everything else do not necessarily want to be hedges. Each hawthorn tree wants to grow tall, to spread its crown over a sturdy, upright trunk. But we humans, especially the farming and gardening variety, want a hedge. So to keep a hedge in a hedge-like shape, maintenance is required. Fortunately, this tends to be beneficial for nesting birds, who find protection and shelter in among the lower thicket of thorny growth.

Without trimming or other management, the hawthorns will revert to their natural tendency to become a line of hawthorn trees. Once this happens, the hedge no longer serves as a stockproof boundary and loses its value on the farm, diminishing a farmer's inclination to retain the hedge. For wildlife too, there is a world of difference between a thick, stockproof hedge and an open, gappy hedge. In some counties where hedgerow surveys have been carried out, an alarmingly high proportion of hedges are open at the base, full of gaps, and are generally in poor condition, both ecologically and agriculturally. Much of our hedgerow resource is in need of renewal. Rejuvenative management techniques, which include hedge laying and coppicing, extend the lifespan of a hedge and can improve both its functionality and its ecological value.

At the other end of the scale is over-management, when hedges are trimmed each year to within an inch of their lives. Keeping a hedge too short and stumpy negates its value for livestock, crops and wildlife. It takes about four years after a stem is cut to set flower and fruit again, so trimming a hedge back each year will limit its flowering and fruiting, and in turn its value to bees, voles, hoverflies, bats, songbirds, owls, kestrels and lots more besides. For many of the 99 species of native bees we have in Ireland, native flowering hedgerow trees and bushes provide protein-rich pollen for bee larvae and energy-giving sustenance for adults.

Planting a Native Hedge

Whether in a garden or along a field boundary, planting a new hedge is always going to be of benefit to wildlife. Choosing native species such as hawthorn, blackthorn, holly, guelder-rose, hazel and spindle will provide habitat for native wildlife.

Looking at which species are growing well in your locality can be a good way to tell which species are suited to the soils where you live and are thus likely to do well. Ideally, the trees and shrubs you plant will also be sourced from a native provenance, rather than imported varieties of the same species. A hawthorn or a holly bred from generations of French hawthorns, for example, will probably burst into flower at a different time than those which have evolved in sync with Irish seasons. This is important when we consider how butterflies, for example, have evolved to time the key stages of their life cycle with the first flush of leaves or flowers. Growing native hedgerow shrubs from seed is also an option if you have the inclination.

Planting climbers such as wild rose and honeysuckle into your hedge adds colour and more opportunities for wildlife, though sourcing native provenance wild roses or honeysuckle can be challenging. Wild honeysuckle is different to the cultivated garden varieties, so for those with green fingers, growing wild honeysuckle or dog rose from cuttings might be worth experimenting with.

Invitations to the Wild Embrace

🍄 Nibble on young hawthorn leaves in spring. They were known as 'bread and butter' in olden times.

🍄 Mark out a stretch of hedgerow and see if you can identify all the different shrubs and trees growing there, including the less well-known species such as spindle and guelder rose.

🍄 Look out for wild honeysuckle clambering over a hedge and take in its scent as dusk descends.

🍄 Plant a native hedge in your garden, school or workplace. In time it will fill up with wildflowers, butterflies, bees, hedgehogs, bats and songbirds, all of whom will appreciate the nesting, feeding and roosting opportunities.

Ladybird in Irish
is *bóin Dé*, 'little
cow of God'

The Small Majority

IKE most children, I had a natural curiosity about
insects. I was fascinated by their intricate little bodies,
intriguing shapes and patterns, their captivating
otherness. I helped my brothers dig up worms for fishing bait.
I remember being enthralled by their squiggly segmented
bodies. I used to collect up dead bees from the corner of the
pond, bringing them home for closer examination.

As we grow up, we are culturally conditioned to dislike
insects. Fear and inconvenience beget prejudice: wasps can
sting, bluebottles are dirty, and slugs and snails eat flowers.
We start to dismiss insects as pests. In not questioning this
prejudice, we deprive our adult selves of our natural curiosity
about the small majority.

Rather than jumping to judgement, we would do well to
question and unlearn the biases we have against insects. We
have so much to gain, personally and ecologically, if we can
adopt a compassionate attitude to these little beings. When

we practise compassion, it tends to reach beyond the intended target. We will likely extend that compassion to ourselves and those around us. Learning to love insects can unleash an attitude of wonder, of seeing beauty in things we tend to overlook or deprecate.

Insects make up more than half of all the animal species in Ireland. Many of them are mind-bogglingly interesting. As well as meriting our curiosity and compassion because of their intrinsic worth, insects are essential to everything. Our entire existence depends on them. Beetles, moths, midges, hoverflies, flies, aphids, shield-bugs, weevils, ants and wasps provide the nutritional mainstay in most food webs; the bulk that is the basis of every ecosystem.

A food chain can be thought of as a triangle rather than a linear chain, with insects, among other things, at the bottom, and just a few larger animals, such as mammals and birds, at the peak near the top. Take away that bottom layer and everything above it disappears too. Other animals such as frogs, bats, badgers, pygmy shrews, mice and hedgehogs all feed on insects and their larvae. Insectivorous birds such as swallows, swifts and house martins feed exclusively on insects, while most of our songbirds depend on insects during the nesting season, when little chicks need a steady supply of protein-rich food in order to survive.

Yet it is not unusual for otherwise enlightened, nature-loving people to reach for ant spray as soon as an ant appears on the garden patio. I'd be far more suspicious of the ant spray than the ant. Without ants, who grow wings in late summer and fly, the swifts we so love to hear screeching overhead would go hungry when they most need sustenance. Waging a war on insects is waging a war on every aspect of nature, because every ecosystem is powered by insects, each with their own niche to fill, their own particular role in the functioning of the whole. If we get anywhere near 'winning' this war, we're all headed for annihilation. I urge you to let go of the fear and learn to love, or at least appreciate, insects, as though your life depends on them – because, in fact, it does!

Our abhorrence for insects wasn't always there. In many cultures, insects were revered as messengers, or literally as a 'god-send'. Ladybirds, for example, can gobble as many as 5,000 greenflies in their lifetime, and for this reason ladybirds are always a welcome addition in market gardens and fields of wheat or barley. In Irish, the name for ladybird is *bóin Dé*, meaning 'little cow of God', a reflection of the medieval belief that ladybirds were sent from the heavens to save food crops from harm. Their red 'cloak' (which are their wing cases) was taken as further evidence of their heavenly edict, as the Virgin Mary herself was at that time commonly depicted as wearing a red cloak. Ladybirds hibernate during the winter months, often gathered *en masse* to share body heat. In autumn, if you see lots of ladybirds huddled together between the joints of fencing posts or in the crevices of an old tree, leave them be, they're sleeping for the winter. Better still, provide additional safe places for ladybirds to hibernate in the garden or on the farm by leaving 'messy' corners. You might be glad you did come spring.

Butterflies

Some butterflies survive the winter by going dormant. Two types of butterfly in Ireland hibernate from October to March.[15] Peacock butterflies and small tortoiseshells fold up their wings and hide away in sheltered nooks and crannies, including unused chimneys, behind wardrobes or picture frames, in sheds or in the cavities of old stone-built walls.

When peacocks and small tortoiseshells emerge from their slumber in spring, they need an energy boost to recharge. Dandelions are often the only thing in flower, making them a crucial resource for these butterflies and other early-emerging insects. Fluffy willow catkins also offer a feed of nectar and pollen for butterflies and bumblebees who make their appearance when there is little else in flower.

Once fed and warmed up, tortoiseshell butterflies gather near nettles where males vie with one another for an opportunity to mate. Willing females lead a high-speed chase, testing the stamina of their potential suitors, before agreeing to dance and then mate. After this, they lay eggs on young nettle leaves. The caterpillars that emerge may not have any parent in sight, but they're surrounded by exactly the right type of leaf which they are specially adapted to eat.

Adult tortoiseshells take sustenance for themselves from thistle flowers, a rich source of nectar for many insects. Luckily for us, nettles and thistles are common plants, which ensures that stunning tortoiseshell butterflies and their iridescent wing patterns are not difficult to observe. Like tortoiseshell caterpillars, peacock butterfly caterpillars live on and eat the leaves of nettles, so these too are a common butterfly.

Iridescent colours are a feature of many insects. Iridescence is when shimmering, living rainbows of light are created by intricate engineering on the body of a beetle, the wings of a fly or the abdomen of a damselfly, or in the elaborate patterns of a butterfly wing. Iridescent colours are not made by pigments, as most colours are, but instead are cast by light waves reflected from several different tiny layers interfering with each other in exactly the right proportion. These are 'structural colours', actively being cast by the careful refractions of light, vividly revealing themselves to those who look from the right direction, like the colours on a soap bubble.

Butterflies' wings are covered in tiny scales, each with colours that combine to form sublime patterns, like a carefully assembled mosaic. Most of the scales are coloured in with vivid pigments, making up the stunningly beautiful patterns on the wings of the fritillary butterflies, for example. Brightly coloured tortoiseshell butterflies have a necklace of iridescent blue spots fringing their orange and black wings, and peacock butterflies have big blue iridescent 'eyespots' on their wings, to fool and thus deter potential predators. Each iridescent scale has carefully placed layers of melanin, air pockets and chitin (a hard substance found in the outer shells of insects). These layers are perfectly sized to divide up minute wavelengths of light and reflect each wavelength in coinciding peaks and troughs, creating the intense glittering reflective blues of the peacock's eyespots.

Butterflies perceive the world differently than we do. Like bees, they have the ability to see ultraviolet light, so when they approach a flower, they see more intricate patterns on the petals than what we can see, guiding them to the nectar at the core of the flower. When a butterfly is prospecting for a good place to lay her eggs, approaching from above on her gorgeous wings, she will use the taste organs on her feet to verify that it's the right food plant before she lays her eggs there. It can be fun to imagine how butterflies and other flying insects see the world, as they glide over radiant flowers of yellow, pink and purple, moving through the air in a more multidimensional realm than we can perceive.

Ants and Aphids

Ants and aphids are not exactly popular with humans, but both have truly fascinating ways of going about their lives. Some species of aphid are pink and live only on the underside of oak leaves; others are light green and live specifically on the underside of birch leaves. Some aphids are commonly known as greenfly or blackfly, but all have a particular way of reproducing.

In spring, all the aphids are female, all are born pregnant, and all give birth within days to live aphid nymphs, who in turn are also pregnant and give birth to another generation of live nymphs. Bear in mind that these little insects are skipping the step, undertaken by most insects, of laying eggs, whilst completely sidestepping the need for sexual reproduction. Instead, virgin females give birth to genetically identical live clones of themselves, right beneath your nose in the rosebush by your garden gate. Males are produced at the end of the summer to ensure that there is some mixing of genes between different populations.

Because aphids suck sap directly from green plants, they contain a lot of sucrose and are a favourite food for ladybirds, beetles, wasps and hoverfly larvae. There is also a twist to the story of their sweetness. The excess sugars that aphids eat are secreted out as a substance called honeydew. It's honeydew that sometimes makes car windscreens or bicycle handlebars sticky in summertime. We might find it a nuisance, but this honeydew is so appealing to ants that they have learned to 'farm' aphids in the same way that we farm cows for their milk. These ants are called 'dairying ants'. The ants protect aphids from predators, bring them to safe places when needed, and even stroke them with their antennae, which raises the protein content of the aphids' sweet secretion.

Bees

A garden in summer would feel strangely vacant without butterflies and bumblebees buzzing about. Bees are now experiencing a moment of fame and popularity. We are rightly fascinated by their role as pollinators and the extraordinary ways in which they organise their hives. Worker bees selflessly devote their lives for the common good of the hive, tirelessly gathering up nectar and pollen to support their queen and all her offspring, their siblings. Bees are renowned for making honey and for living in highly organised social colonies.

What this portrayal of bees misses out on is that the majority of the species do not make honey and are not even social. Worldwide, a whopping 95 per cent of bees are solitary species who don't live in colonies and have no need for honey. In Ireland, of the 99 species of native bee species, 80 are solitary bees.

Solitary bees don't always look the way we expect bees to look. Some are slender and black; others look more like wasps than bees. The mason bee has tinges of blue. They don't need big nests like colony-forming bumblebees do; instead, they often avail of existing cavities amongst plants, such as the hollow stem of a reed. For others, a small hole in a stone wall or sandy bank makes a perfect nesting site. One species of solitary bee in Ireland makes a nest in empty snail shells among sand dunes. Leaf-cutter bees have learnt to slice out circles from leaves and use them like plywood boards to shelter their little nests. Each species has a unique approach to life.

Solitary bees are excellent pollinators. Some are even more efficient at pollinating crops and apple orchards than bumblebees or honeybees. When solitary bees lay eggs, they tend to leave a little pile of pollen for when the larvae hatch. Once the larvae have eaten all the pollen left for them by their absent parent, they spend the winter safely tucked away as a cocoon, emerging the following spring or summer as a fully formed bee.

The much-celebrated honeybee is not a native species to Ireland. Honeybees were most likely first brought here by early Christian monastics, valuable for both their honey and their wax. One type of honeybee, a black bee, is often referred to as native, and although they have been here a long time, they are not native in an ecological sense. Like other domesticated creatures, they are bred for their produce and survive the winter because we help them to do so. Honeybees originate in warmer climes where they need large stores of honey for overwintering. Our native bees, on the other hand, mostly die off for the winter. This means that they have no need to make big stores of honey. Only a few queens born late in the summer survive the cold of winter, slowing their metabolism during the coldest months and emerging in spring to begin a new colony.

Since the beginning of the 21st century, many of Ireland's native bees are struggling to survive. Where there were meadows and wildflower-rich habitats, now there are intensively managed fields of ryegrass and manicured lawns. Soils are compacted by heavy machinery and nesting opportunities are rare. Many hedges are trimmed too far back each year to have an opportunity to flower. A scarcity of wildflowers in the landscape means bees go hungry. Our collective cultural preference is for tightly managed parks and gardens, favouring sterile lawns and exotic trees and shrubs over flower-rich meadows, native trees and flowering bushes. With these inclinations for neatness and control, we are depriving wild bees and butterflies of both food and shelter.

As a result, over half of Ireland's native bees have suffered substantial declines since 1980, when monitoring began. Almost one third of wild bee species are considered threatened with extinction here. Similar rates of decline are being recorded for butterflies too. In just 10 years, from 2008 to 2018, there were 6 per cent fewer butterflies flying around Irish habitats. This is an enormous decline in such a short space of time. The consequences of allowing this trajectory to continue are unfathomable. Making space for bees and butterflies is a joyful act, an empowering response to an alarming situation. We can encourage nectar-rich flowers at every opportunity, leave wildflower verges and lawns to grow, and make space for natural habitats and semi-natural grasslands in the wider countryside. Actions that help bees have beneficial impacts on lots of other species, too.

Unsung Heroes

Ladybirds, butterflies and bumblebees are some of the more charismatic insects; species that we readily admit to liking. But there are thousands of other insects – upwards of 11,000 different species in Ireland alone – who get barely any attention. Yet without these little creatures, life on earth would collapse.

Beneath the ground, down among the tree roots, mingling with mycorrhizal fungi, hundreds of invertebrates spend their entire lives carrying out essential services to which we rarely pay heed. Earthworms burrowing in the soil chomp through dead leaves and detritus, mixing organic matter with crystalline minerals from fragments of rock, making perfect compost that sustains all the plants growing above. Powered by five tiny hearts, each earthworm is a self-sustaining fund of fertility that all of us benefit from. Earthworms are so significant in maintaining soil structure and fertility that Charles Darwin was obsessed with them, spending 40 years researching and writing a book called *The Formation of Vegetable Mould through the Action of Worms*.

Together with microscopic micro-organisms, invertebrates such as millipedes, mites, springtails, grubs, nematodes, worms, woodlice, slugs and tiny snails are unseen at work, breaking down minerals and recycling dead plant matter, relentlessly returning nutrients to the soil. These unsung heroes are known as 'the decomposers', and while it's not a glamourous role, we'd be lost without them.

Pressure Relief

There is much we can do to help insects. In wintertime, some need places to hibernate in safety until next spring. Whether at home or in the workplace, leaving little nooks and crannies about the garden, in the gaps of garden walls, or amid a pile of logs, offers safe places for ladybirds and butterflies to overwinter.

Where there are lawns, minimising mowing to later in the summer will create habitat for grasshoppers, bees and butterflies. Giving wild plants the chance to flower and set seed offers a kindness to all insect life. With a little change of mindset, accommodating wildflowers and their insect allies in our outdoor spaces can bring unexpected rewards. I've been awed by the arrival of wild orchids in my garden where I had never seen them before, simply by not mowing until the end of the summer. I now hear grasshoppers singing throughout August, a wonderful prompt to pause and listen, to hover for the chance to see these cryptically coloured creatures. Allowing lawns to revert to meadows brings out colours and textures that are far more pleasing to the eye than a manicured monoculture of homogenous green.

Making space for native trees is another way to loosen our control. Birch, willow, hazel, rowan, holly, crab apple and wild cherry are all native trees that don't get too big, so are well suited to gardens. These native trees support a huge diversity of life. As well as hosting insects, they provide shelter to the swifts, swallows, house martins and bats who swoop about the garden in a feeding frenzy every summer evening.

The biggest challenges to insects are occurring in the wider countryside, where once flower-rich fields are being replaced with more intensive ryegrass pastures, left bereft of diversity and dependent on fertilisers. Wetlands are being drained away to make more room for ryegrass fields and plantations of spruce. There is little space for invertebrates in intensively managed farmland or plantations made up of only one or two non-native tree species. Bees are one of the few species groups we have information for, and we know that many of our bees are starving and homeless, struggling to survive.

There is some hope in that most insects produce a lot of offspring. If we can restore enough habitats and provide connectivity through the landscape, many insect populations have a good chance of bouncing back.

Observing Insects

Insects have surprising shapes, colours and textures. They can be beautiful and weird. If you have an interest in identifying insect species, it is worth getting yourself a zoom monocular –

a small magnifier that is used with one eye. More commonly, these are used by hikers, hunters and soldiers to see clearly over long distances, but a monocular with a zoom is a wonderful way to look at details of butterflies and bees without having to get too close and risk frightening them off. With a zoom monocular, you can hover by a calm lakeshore in summertime and zoom in on the shimmering colours and helicopter-like wings of a dragonfly in the rushes by the lake edge, or perhaps even spot a damselfly emerging from their casing on the bulrushes – metamorphosis in action.

Invitations to the Wild Embrace

❦ Learn to recognise a few of the butterflies that you see regularly. Try to spot the difference between bees and their hoverfly mimics.

❦ Let dandelions grow! These are one of the most important food plants for pollinators in spring.

❦ If you have a garden, make it attractive to insects by leaving messy wild corners where all sorts of plants offer food, shelter and hibernating sites. Even a small area of long grass will provide a refuge for many insects and other small creatures.

❦ Listen out for grasshoppers in high summer.

❦ Get involved in a citizen science monitoring project with the National Biodiversity Data Centre, which runs training and events for monitoring bumblebees, dragonflies and other invertebrate groups.

❦ Don't use chemicals such as slug pellets, ant spray or any pesticides. However carefully you use them, they will kill a wide range of insects, not just the few you are targeting.

Astonishing
findings reveal
a world of
cooperation

Symbiosis

I T is well established that symbiosis is central to how
nature works. Symbiosis can be broadly described as the
intimate association of two or more species.[16] It is intrinsic to every plant, animal and fungus everywhere, including
us. But scientific research is now revealing that symbiotic
relationships, often mutually beneficial ones, have been central
to the development of life on land and are core to the healthy
functioning of every ecosystem on earth. The extent to which
organisms are involved in each other's lives is nothing short of
mindboggling, upturning our perceptions of whether there is
such a thing as a 'species' or an 'individual' at all.

Some of the most exciting revelations that have been
unfolding in science in recent times involve the degree
of connectedness between different lifeforms, from the
microbiome in our gut to fungal mycorrhiza[17] connecting
entire forest systems. Our understanding of the extent to
which major planetary systems are driven by these biological
interactions is also rapidly developing. We are learning what

a key role symbiosis plays in soil formation and fertility, carbon cycling, atmospheric composition, climate and ocean currents. We could even go so far as to say that new understandings of symbiotic relationships between organisms are redefining how life on earth exists, from a microscopic scale of interactions right up to a planetary scale. Finely tuned reciprocal interactions between plants and animals power the components of every environmental system.

Lichens

The term symbiosis was coined in 1887 to describe the living partnership of fungi and algae together as a lichen. Each lichen is not an organism in itself, but a cohabiting arrangement between a fungus and an algae. The fungus provides the physical structure and a moist environment in which algal cells can grow and photosynthesise. The fungus also digests minuscule bits of mineral from the rock or tree it grows on, handing these nutrients over to its partner, the algae. The algal cells provide compounds that feed the fungi, which unlike the algae, have no chlorophyll and are unable to generate their own food. Because of the collaborating symbiotic relationship that is a lichen, these organisms are capable of incredible achievements, including living extraordinarily long lives.

Here in Ireland, lichens can be seen just about everywhere. There are probably several different lichen species growing within metres of where you are now. They are the colourful clumps and scaly clusters growing on rocks, stone walls, cement surfaces, roof slates, tree trunks, fence posts, gravestones and monuments. They are the little blobs of white on your patio stone, like drops of spilled paint. Lichens come in many colours: yellow, orange, lime, white, green, black, brown, grey and everything in between. Each of the 1,200 known species of lichen in Ireland are unique in their habitat preferences.

Walls made of stone and mortar will normally have several types of lichen patterning the surface, anchoring to the rock as circles of white and yellow. Some are surprisingly smooth, and others look like sprinklings of colourful powder. Roofing tiles and slates will be colonised with lichens after just a few years. Even the concrete pillars of a farm gate or an urban car park will accumulate several types of lichen with time, depending on the chemical components of the concrete and the character of the surrounding environment.

Trees, including those growing in urban streets and parks, are populated with several types of lichen. Some species prefer to live in the crevices of the bark, whereas others dangle from small twigs high up the tree. Some lichens look like flattened coral, while others grow as bulbous jelly-like blobs. Particularly characterful are the pale green clumps that branch out like pom-poms of tiny antlers, hanging in clumps from the twigs of sycamore trees. Because the bark of each different tree species has a specific acidity level (its pH), there are lichens that grow only on a particular type of tree. Hazel trees, for example, have lichens living on their smooth golden rods that won't be found growing on the bark of holly or oak. Lichens also have particular preferences for east-facing or west-facing, humid or dry, and so on.

Some species grow as tangled shaggy bundles among the hummocks of heather in wet boggy fields. *Cladonia* are a group of crunchy lichens whose reproductive, spore-bearing parts are held aloft on a stalk, enchantingly turning themselves bright red when the spores are ripe. Some *cladonia* species produce protruding trumpet-shaped wine goblets that look perfectly suited to a 4-centimetre-tall pixie. These species are variously called pixie cup and elf cup lichen.

At the coast, rocky shorelines are dramatically populated with lichens. Bright yellow mats of yellow leafy lichen mingle with shaggy pale grey-green tufts of sea ivory, which look like miniature twiggy clumps that someone has artfully arranged. Black tar lichen also occupies the splash zone on coastal rocks; its smooth circular shapes could be mistaken for splodges of black tarry paint on the rock surface.

It's easy to go through life without ever really taking notice of lichens, but once you begin to look, you will soon see them everywhere. Lichens are worth looking at through a hand lens or a magnifying glass, so you can observe their variety of psychedelic, otherworldly shapes and forms.

There is a common conception that the presence of lichens is a sign of good air quality, but this is not strictly true. While many lichens *are* sensitive to air pollution and are intolerant of ammonia – a gaseous by-product of nitrogen fertilisers – there are lichens who can manage just fine with high levels of pollution. Some lichens can even tolerate high levels of radioactivity. After the Chernobyl nuclear disaster, lichens were found growing near the reactors, demonstrating their ability to withstand nuclear radiation. There are lichens living in the driest parts of deserts and lichens that prosper in Antarctica. Lichens have even managed to survive in space. These little fungi have developed partnerships that have adapted to fit in literally every niche on earth, an approach that also allows them to withstand the most extreme conditions.

Because lichens are mostly made up of fungi, they are considered part of the kingdom of fungi. Since 2016 it has been discovered that most lichens are not, as previously thought, made up of one species of fungus and one species of algae. Instead, most lichens have several species living together as symbionts, and they often associate with bacteria too. The more that scientists look at lichens, the more these wondrous lifeforms defy our definition of species.

Time is the other arena where lichens challenge our ideas of what a lifespan can be. The collaborative approach adopted by lichens is clearly a successful strategy. The oldest known lichen is more than 9,000 years old, in Sweden. In Ireland, there are plenty of lichens growing on big old rocks that are probably 5,000 years old or more. One example is *Rhizocarpon geographicum*, which grows on granite rock in coastal and upland locations. When you are next up in the mountains, resting on a big granite boulder with a flask of tea, you might be perched beside a lichen that was growing happily in the very same spot, all the way back when a Neolithic hunter paused at the boulder to adjust the flint on her arrowhead, after having just missed an attempt on a wild boar.

Competition and Cooperation

Traditional views of how nature works have, for centuries, been overemphasising the role of competition, which in turn has influenced the dominant frame through which we see, and shape, the world. The belief that competition is 'the natural order of things' has pervaded politics, economics, agriculture and much else besides. Rigid misinterpretations of Darwin's theory of evolution portray the natural world as a 'survival of the fittest', in which all living organisms are essentially in competition with each other. Of course, competition exists, and Darwin described it as one of the major factors determining how each species evolves. However, he was also clear that each organism's ability to adapt to a niche is at least as strong a determinant as competition in terms of how species evolve. Recent scientific discoveries about the extraordinary degree of collaboration and cooperation between organisms are fundamentally changing our perception of how the natural world works.

There are native orchids growing in the wild all over Ireland which have special symbiotic relationships with a species of fungus. Underground in the soil, the seeds of these orchids need the presence of this fungus in order to germinate. As the orchid seedlings grow into healthy flowering orchid plants, they are assisted by tiny threads of fungus drawing in carbon and other nutrients to the plants' root tips. Later, when the plant is well established, the orchid supplies the fungus with energy it has made through photosynthesis. Without each other, neither orchid nor fungus would survive. If the ground is sprayed with fertilisers or pesticides, the fungus dies off, meaning the orchids will soon disappear from that site. This is why most orchid species are highly sensitive to the drainage, ploughing and reseeding of fields, and why orchid-rich meadows, common across Ireland only 30 years ago, have become such a rare treat to find.

Some orchids take their relationship with fungi a step further. Bird's-nest orchids grow in oak and other native deciduous woodland. These orchids are eerie looking, like ghosts of an orchid, as they contain no chlorophyll at all and thus are incapable of photosynthesis. This is a strange predicament for a plant. Instead, bird's-nest orchids depend on underground entanglements with tiny threads of fungus for their nutrition throughout their lives. In return, the fungus gets shelter and other as yet unknown benefits.

It's not just orchids who have critical relationships with

fungi. An astonishing 90 per cent of all plants depend on fungi, in similar ways to those we have understood of orchids for some time. Plants photosynthesise, and produce glucose and carbon-based compounds which are shared with the fungi, who in turn provide phosphorus, nitrogen and other nutrients that they are better at absorbing from the soil than plant roots are.

Both plants and animals have symbiotic relationships with bacteria, too. Alder, for example, a common native tree right across Ireland, is generally looked upon as a 'weed' by many, because of its ability to seed itself and grow well in even the soggiest, heaviest land. Alder trees have a secret superpower, enabling them to thrive in conditions that most trees would struggle in. They can draw in atmospheric nitrogen and transform it into bioavailable nutrients. The secret behind this superpower of alder trees is a special relationship with 'nitrogen-fixing' bacteria that live in nodules on the their roots.

Nitrogen gas makes up 78 per cent of the earth's atmosphere, but most plants are unable to absorb nitrogen in this gaseous form. This is because nitrogen atoms adhere very tightly to one another, a triple-strength molecular bond that requires huge energy to break.

Nitrogen is the primary component of proteins that both plants and animals need to grow and repair cells. We humans only discovered how to break the nitrogen bond in 1903 through a chemical process that requires enormous quantities of heat and energy and is now used to manufacture bombs and artificial fertilisers, among other things. But some species of bacteria figured out how to break this bond early in their evolution, a process known as nitrogen fixing. A few (though not many) plants have figured out how to live in symbiosis with these nitrogen-fixing bacteria and thus benefit from direct delivery of nitrogen straight to their root systems without any major effort. Alder trees are one such species.

There is an alder tree growing in front of my house, which seeded itself in an old tin pot 12 years ago. It is now a 20-metre-tall tree, home to a constant chorus of starlings and great tits, and an assortment of tiny flying insects which provide sustenance for the swallows, swifts, house martins and bats who are so plentiful in and about the house and garden. These creatures bring us so much joy to see and listen to on summer days, especially in the evening time when we sit out to watch the landscape in the fading evening light. To me, this alder tree represents the strength drawn from symbiotic relationships.

Gunnera, a giant-leaved rhubarb-like plant that is now an invasive species along the western seaboard, also has special nitrogen-fixing bacteria living in its roots. All the legumes have this advantage too – wild peas that we call vetch, garden peas, chickpeas, kidney beans, soybeans, lentils and even peanuts are rich in protein only because these plants have a symbiotic relationship with nitrogen-fixing bacteria in their roots. These legumes provide essential protein intake for most human vegetarians.

Root Relationships

While it has long been understood that trees send airborne signals to each other (to warn of incoming pest attacks, for example), the degree of communication between trees in a forest ecosystem through fungal channels is now a major new frontier of research. Scientific understanding of connectivity and communications between trees in woodland ecosystems has revealed that mycorrhizal networks are actively connecting trees in a woodland and facilitating an exchange of lots of different compounds between trees connected into the network.[18] In a mycorrhizal association, the microscopic threads of fungi inhabit the root tips of plants and trees and also extend out into immense networks that grow from tree roots in the surrounding soil.

These subterranean fungal filaments absorb mineral nutrients from their surrounds and pass on these nutrients to the trees by connecting directly with the cells in their roots. The trees in turn provide the fungi with carbohydrates which they cannot produce themselves, because, as we have noted previously, fungi do not have the ability to photosynthesise.

Incredible findings since the 1990s have revealed that not only do the mycorrhizal fungi exist in symbiosis with the trees they connect with, but they also provide the means of communication and transportation between different trees. From the perspective of the fungi, these connections allow them to occupy enormous areas and gain access to a large number of plant partners.

Parent trees can be connected through this network to young saplings far away. Alder trees, with the assistance of the nitrogen-fixing bacteria in their roots, can send nitrogen to other trees in the woodland, to species such as oak and pine who do not have the bacterial symbionts capable of transforming nitrogen into bioavailable forms. Evergreen trees sometimes send supplementary nutrients to broadleaved trees in spring, a helping boost when the trees haven't yet grown fresh leaves. Later in the season, these broadleaved trees supply nutrients to the conifers that they are connected to via the mycorrhizal network.

These associations are invisible to us; we cannot see the connections. Fungi are made up mostly of extremely fine underground filaments, channelling chemical compounds through tiny tubes, existing in a complex, dynamic and responsive mesh that constitutes the organism. The mushrooms that we see growing above ground are the fruiting bodies of these fungi, like apple blossom and apples produced by apple trees. Mushrooms are the reproductive organs of fungi, emerging above ground to produce and disperse spores.[19] We are now finding out that fungi comprise as much as a quarter of the world's biomass, but because most of this is underground, in threads too fine for us observe with the naked eye, we know and understand very little of how these fungi work.

These relationships between species challenge established commercial forestry practices, which have long regarded alder as a weed that must be exterminated from young plantations, often with heavy loads of herbicides. Now we are learning that the resilience of whole forest ecosystems is strengthened by the relationships between trees of different ages and species and underground fungi. Healthy trees supply weaker trees with water and other compounds, transported through networks, sustaining those trees who are suffering from drought, for example. Scientists are beginning to understand the importance of mycorrhizal symbionts in trees' abilities to tolerate all kinds of stress. Trees that grow as part of a connected network will be better able to survive frequent droughts and other challenges caused by climate change.

In Ireland, there is very little research about fungi and their mycorrhizal associations with trees and other plants. However, from studies in other countries, we know that the very conspicuous red and white fly agaric mushroom forms symbiotic mycorrhizal relationships with the root tips of birch and other woodland trees. Rather than a collection of competing individuals, trees and fungi are operating in complex and dynamic symbiosis as a cohesive, adaptable and resilient system.

Astonishing findings are revealing a world of cooperation as well as competition, and that trees have 'memory', and are capable of the collective sharing of resources between many interconnected trees in a forest. These discoveries are overturning long-held assumptions about competition as the main stimulus within ecosystems. Ecology has much to teach us about the value of community, connection and resilience.

The Human Microbiome

Recent discoveries about mutual cooperation, healing and resilience in forest ecosystems have implications for how we perceive ourselves as individual organisms who live separately from nature and from each other. While new understandings of the interconnectedness of natural ecosystems unfold in science labs across the world, we are also discovering how much our own bodies are in symbiosis with other organisms. Our digestion and immunity are reliant on a whole host of organisms who live in and on our bodies (collectively known as the 'human microbiome'), without which we wouldn't survive for long.

In the 1950s and '60s, my maternal grandfather, a medical doctor, did a great deal of research on the role of bacteria in our gut. He made some groundbreaking discoveries about how having a healthy community of these organisms was essential for our immune systems and general health. My mum often described how her father was ostracised from the medical community for pursuing this field of research. He was being outspoken about findings that challenged the medical understanding of the importance of 'other' organisms present in our bodies. It was decades before our dependence on a healthy gut microbiome became generally accepted. This dependence is only now becoming common knowledge, with enormous ramifications for both mental and physical health.

In our gut, it is communities of bacteria who do the work of absorbing nutrients from the food we eat. Without them, we would be incapable of digestion. We think of ourselves as individuals, preferring to overlook that 'our' bodies are comprised of more microbial cells than human cells. Every part of our body is teeming with bacterial and fungal cells, not just in our gut, but also on and in our skin, ears, eyes, and every organ and orifice. We are entirely dependent on this microbiome.

I never met my grandfather, as he died before I was born. I often wonder, were my grandfather still alive, what he would make of the daily discoveries in this new frontier of knowledge, proving our total dependence on symbiotic relationships with the bacteria in our bodies. I imagine that he would have been amazed to follow – and even have had the chance to participate in – revelations that have transformed our understanding of symbiosis. He would have been awed by the knowledge that we, too, are a shared pool of species, a collection of cohabiting

organisms. There is no such thing in any plant or animal –
including us – as a separate, stand-alone individual.

Zooming out from the scale of our bodies, we are also
dependent on the plethora of symbiotic relationships that are
core to healthy, functioning ecosystems.

Invitations to the Wild Embrace

❦ Examine an old stone wall for lichens. Use a hand lens or magnifying glass to observe their strange shapes and forms.

❦ Look out for the beautiful flower heads and distinctive leaf patterns of wild peas in hedge banks, woodlands and gardens. Recall how these plants have special bacteria living in little nodules in their roots which fix nitrogen, making it available for the plant to use; this is why peas and other legumes are so rich in protein.

❦ Look out for conspicuous red and white fly agaric mushrooms in an autumn woodland. Bring to mind the subterranean mycorrhizal relationships they form with the root tips of birch and other woodland trees.

❦ Next time you eat live yoghurt or natural sauerkraut, thank the microscopic bacteria for helping to support your healthy gut microbiome.

Mosses and
lichens crowd
branches
and twigs

Luminous Woods

LOOK up into the green solar sink of a leafy tree. Each layer of the canopy is efficiently engineered to maximise productivity, every leaf perfectly placed to capture light spilling down directly from the sun. Because the overhead arrangement of leaves is different in each type of tree, gazing up into the canopy of an oak reveals a different leaf pattern to that of an ash, a birch or a willow tree.

In a woodland we get to experience what it feels like to be inside the body of a living, breathing ecosystem, where each element is cohesively entwined. Mosses crowd the branches. Lichens colonise twigs. Shiny mats of liverwort line shady stream sides. Spiders spin webs to capture winged insects passing through. Clambering stems of ivy piggyback on the structural strength of taller trees. By seeking out every opportunity for climbing space, their tangle of stems and evergreen leaves offer shelter for roosting bats by day and for sleeping birds by night; as well as sweet nectar for insects in the autumn. Scientists are now beginning to refer to each woodland as an organism in its own right, such is the degree of interdependent relationships between the various components. When we enter these ecosystems, we inhale the oxygen produced by the plants as they breathe in our respired carbon dioxide.

The experience of being inside woodland, wrapped up in such lusciousness, has been shown to stimulate our brains and prompt the production of pleasure-inducing compounds. We look around and see trees in every direction; dappled golden green beams of light, trunks towering above, intertwining twigs, leaves and gangly saplings beside us, and the fractal shapes of ferns hanging from boulders and branches at every level. Around our ankles are the long leaves of woodrush, spiked sedge and the leaves and stems of flowering plants: bluebell, wood anemone, wood sorrel and occasional orchids.

This is a description of a healthy, native, deciduous woodland, the climax habitat of Ireland and most of Europe too. Since the time of our earliest ancestor hominids millions of years ago, humans have been evolving alongside trees. We depend on trees as much as we depend on our lungs, so it is little wonder that there is such solace in the green-tinged light and shelter of an overhead canopy of leaves. The mossy, earthy smells are made by molecules that tap into ancient parts of our brains, where scent is connected to memory. Here we remember where we came from; the woodlands where, for most of human history, we were at home.

In a wooded setting we are enveloped, stimulated and

sheltered by layers of living texture and colour, protected from wind and rain. The sights and sounds of the world beyond are filtered out. Our ears attune to the rustle of leaves and the scuttle of blackbirds in the undergrowth. Jays screech loudly as they expertly manoeuvre thorugh branches and boles; woodpeckers thrum on tree trunks. While we don't necessarily hear the hypersonic squeaks of long-nosed shrews foraging for bugs among moss-covered boulders and fallen logs, these are part of the woodland soundscape too.[20]

Beneath our feet are the unseen roots, rocks and bustling world of millions of microscopic creatures, who are busy breaking down and recombining matter, recycling nutrients through the whole living system. A gargantuan quantity of unseen organisms are enmeshed with each other and with all the larger, visible woodland plants and animals. We are part of these systems too, so re-familiarising ourselves with the sights, sounds and smells can help us to feel more connected. Touching leaves and mosses with our fingers, we feel their textures. Going barefoot in the tangle offers a tactile connection too. I love finding hazelnuts or acorns in my coat pockets that remind me of my excursions amongst the trees they came from.

Spring Flowers

In springtime, woodlands are abuzz with kinetic energy as every living component prepares to burst into action for the season ahead. Looking up into the bare branches above, leaf buds are just beginning to emerge. Underfoot, the rich brown leaf litter from the previous autumn has been churned and chomped by an array of decomposers: the bacteria, fungi, mites, millipedes, earthworms and nematodes who have kindly created the perfect rich brown soil for saplings and spring flowers to emerge through. Every organism in a natural woodland is embroiled in a web of mutual support.

Bluebells, wild garlic, wood anemones, violets and wood sorrel respond to the lengthening days and strengthening light, knowing that their window of time to make the most of the sunlight is limited. Soon the bigger canopy trees will have a fresh covering of leaves that will cast a shade on the woodland floor. Woodland plants have evolved special strategies to speed-start their growth early each spring. Bluebells, before going dormant for winter, sequester away stores of energy as bulbs in the soil below. After spring equinox, when temperatures begin to rise and days lengthen, bluebells begin a turbo-powered spurt of growth. Their fairy bell flowers offer a welcome early feast of nectar for new bumblebee queens who are just emerging from hibernation.

Wild garlic uses the same strategy to be able to flower so early in the year, storing away energy over winter in the bulbous base that we know as wild garlic roots. Foragers are always enthusiastic about wild garlic, and April is when eager instagrammers show off their wild garlic pesto at every online opportunity. In traditional folk medicine, wild garlic is recommended to boost the immune system, purify the blood and keep colds and coughs at bay.

Badgers use their long claws to dig out bluebell and wild garlic bulbs. Their scrapes are often visible on the woodland floor in spring. Little wood mice nibble on these bulbs too, for good starchy sustenance when other fruits, nuts and seeds are mostly unavailable.

Wood sorrel is an easy plant to recognise. Its leaves are shamrock-shaped and its flowers are a delicate white, standing out amongst all the spring greens. Wood anemones also have bright white flowers, though theirs are star-shaped and filled with pollen-laden yellow anthers. Lesser celandine has shimmering yellow flowers. Like other buttercup species, its petals have layers of bright yellow pigment overlain with a thin film of minutely engineered air chambers that catch and reflect light to give off a glossy reflective shimmer.

Blossoming in May and June, wild violets are essential in the life cycle of silver-washed fritillary butterflies, whose stunning, orange-patterned wings can be seen carrying them through sunny openings in the woodland or soaking up the summer sunshine on a hazel leaf. Silver-washed fritillaries lay their eggs in the grooves of tree bark, directly above wild violet plants. Once the eggs hatch, the caterpillars spend the winter on the tree trunk, hibernating there until spring arrives. When the violets spread their little heart-shaped leaves in spring, the caterpillars descend upon them to feed.

Tree Sex

Dainty flowers growing on the woodland floor are not the only blossoms in a woodland in spring. Trees flower too. We don't think of oak and ash as producing flowers, but they also need to make pollen with which to fertilise female flowers in order to make seeds and reproduce. Because so many deciduous trees rely on the wind to transport their pollen, they have no need for pretty-coloured petals or pleasing smells. The wind is much less discerning than a bee or a butterfly. Wind-pollinated plants can afford to be a bit more pragmatic; thus ash trees produce flowers that are tiny, dark purple spangly things, designed to dangle in the wind and let the pollen loose. Ash flowers appear in April and May, to ensure they get their job done before layers of woodland leaves would hinder the dispersal of pollen on the breeze.

Oak trees also produce small, subtle flowers in spring. Hundreds of tiny blossoms are held in tumbling tassels of golden green that we call catkins. Hazel has bright golden-yellow catkins, a beautiful sight in early spring. Their yellow colour comes from the millions of tiny grains of pollen that each catkin produces, to raise the odds of a few grains happening to chance upon a female flower of another tree. In hazel, the male flowers grow as catkins and the female flowers grow separately. The female flowers are tiny sparks of bright crimson, so small that you could walk past them every day and never notice them.

Willow trees also erupt with thousands of fluffy catkins, noticeably abuzz with bees and other insects in early spring. Unlike other trees, willow hedges its bets with pollination, using both animals and the wind for dispersal. Female catkins produce nectar, a reward for bees who might visit with an accidental load of pollen from another willow tree. Willow catkins provide one of the main food sources for early-emerging insects, who need their protein-rich pollen for nutrition and their sugar-rich nectar for an energy boost in the cold of February and March, when little else is flowering and the insects' foraging options are limited. Over thousands of years of co-evolution, early-emerging bumblebee queens and willow catkins have synchronised their emergence; the feeding frenzy is always a delight to happen upon.

Once the genes of two trees have successfully fused, a seed begins to develop. Each tree needs a strategy to get the ripened seeds out into the world. Willow trees, who have a pioneering approach to life, have seeds that are minute, light and equipped with fine hairs to carry them off on the wind. Ash 'keys' or seeds have wings to help them flutter away from the parent tree. Oak and hazel trees have a different approach, having chosen instead to recruit the help of larger animals to spread their seeds. Acorns and hazelnuts are packed with nutrients, proteins and fats, thus are nutritious fodder for squirrels. Jays are woodland birds who specialise in eating acorns. Each autumn, these creatures carry lots of acorns and hazelnuts off, stashing away a plentiful supply to last them through the winter. Inevitably, some get forgotten and sprout from the spot where they were accidentally 'planted' by these helpful woodland animals.

But having animals who are so fond of your seeds can be problematic, too. If all the seeds are eaten, or even almost all, there will be little chance of ample seedlings sprouting, so trees have found a clever way to outmanoeuvre the squirrels and the jays. Every few years, oak and hazel, along with other trees who depend on animals to disperse their seeds, have what is called a 'mast year'. In the case of oak, for example, all the trees in the region synchronise with each other to flower profusely and produce a glut of acorns that year, intentionally making far more than all he jays and squirrels could possibly consume. This guarantees that a portion of the excess acorns will be forgotten about by the squirrels and jays who stash them away.

Mast years only happen every few years, maybe three years apart, maybe seven. They are always intentionally unpredictable, to make sure that the populations of squirrels and jays do not grow to such an extent that they could consume all the excess acorns. The most impressive thing about this strategy, apart from being so clever, is how all the trees in a region plan in advance (when the flowers are produced in early spring), coordinating with each other to make this irregular occurrence a success by involving every oak tree in the region. Once again, we see that no tree acts as an individual.

The Next Generation

In a healthy deciduous woodland, the structure is neither laid out on a grid nor limited to trees who are all the same age. One of the loveliest things about being enveloped in the leafiness of a wild woodland is being surrounded by trees at every stage of life, where the recruits for the next generation are mingling with their elders and natural regeneration is clearly manifest.

Here saplings emerge amongst old trees, protected by thickets of thorny bramble that keep predators at bay, like any good nursery attendant. Saplings grow tall and spindly with only a few scant leaves to show for themselves. While under the shade of mature canopy trees, light is a limiting factor. Often understorey trees grow slowly for many more years than their size would suggest, flexible and resilient, reaching out laterally to bathe their leaves in the few dappled pools of light available. They are preparing well for the possibility of a long life. During this time, the mature trees are not entirely greedy. The older generation, often parent trees, nurture the young and the struggling, sharing nutrients via fungal root connections.

When a big branch comes down from overhead, or an ageing tree reaches the end of its life, a gap opens up in the canopy. Saplings flooded with light for the first time in their lives grow rapidly, reaching to secure a place at the top. A healthy woodland will always have taller canopy trees, such as oak and ash, sheltering saplings, alongside small trees such as hazel, holly, birch, rowan, spindle and hawthorn.

It is only in plantations that we constrain the essentially social character of trees, planting just one or two tree species, arranging them in evenly spaced rows, allowing no room for diversity or natural interactions. Most plantations are fraudulent forests, void of the throng of life that characterises a woodland, where every nook and cranny is habitat to some specially adapted plant or creature.

In many woodlands in Ireland, overgrazing is an existential problem. Young trees are obliterated when there is an overabundance of deer, goats and sheep, who chew at bark and thus prevent trees from being able to transport water up from their roots and sugars down from their leaves. Saplings get nibbled to death before they have a chance to reach for the top. In overgrazed woodlands, there are no new trees to be the next generation; this puts the whole ecosystem in jeopardy. When you know what you're not seeing, it is easy to spot an absence of the saplings that should be filling every available space beneath the canopy. This is the reason why many deciduous woods are fenced – to keep deer and other browsers out, a necessary protection if the woodlands are to survive.

When wolves roamed free across Ireland, deer were always on the move, never lingering long in one place. Now deer have no natural predators and are free to munch at leisure on every sapling that might otherwise offer hope for the ongoing process of woodland regeneration.

Living Lungs

Each layer of green leaves that makes up a thriving woodland is a feast for our senses. Inside a wild wood just before dawn, the feeling of kinetic energy is tangible, as every tiny grain of chlorophyll in every leaf is switching gear, readying for the sunlight. By the time the sun rises, each leafy receptor is angled to absorb the endless stream of photons coming directly from the sun. These tiny packets of energy excite the leaves' chlorophyll into action. The magical chlorophyll molecules suck in air and water, breaking hydrogen away from oxygen to recombine the atoms with carbon, concocting carbohydrates, sugars, proteins and fats, and spewing out oxygen as they weave life from the light of the sun.

The compounds that leaves create nourish the tree, enabling roots to penetrate deeper and branches to reach further. They also sustain aphids, ants, speckled wood butterflies, solitary bees, shield-bugs, moths, pipistrelle bats, shrews, chaffinches, thrushes, squirrels, badgers, sparrowhawks and long-eared owls, to name but a few. As we've already emphasised (it's worth repeating): woodlands are the culmination of life on this island, the natural climax habitat of this latitude, what almost every acre in Ireland still strives to be.[21]

The oxygen that is a by-product of all this energetic tree action is what endows everything else on earth with the gift of life. We have woodlands to thank for being the lungs of the earth. Yet we in Ireland have deemed these ecosystems worthy of less than two per cent of the land area.[22] A further nine per cent is covered in plantations, mostly comprised of uniform rows of conifers. The planting, maintenance and cycle of clear-felling involved in managing these conifer plantations has earned them the dubious accolade of being amongst the leading drivers of biodiversity loss in Ireland over the past 40 years.

We tend to blame the lack of tree cover in Ireland on colonial clearances, but after a century of independence, we still have the lowest proportion of forest cover in Europe (except for Malta). Remaining pockets of native woodland are small and fragmented, confined to the steep slopes and inaccessible gorges that made clearance too challenging. Even these fragments are barely managing to survive the onslaught of invasive species and browsing by deer, sheep and goats.

With climate change accelerating and biodiversity severely depleted, restoring and expanding each fragment of remaining native woodland has never been more urgent. There is no great technical challenge in allowing trees to seed themselves: keep browsing animals and invasive species away from tender saplings, and provide corridors for connectivity through the landscape. Given our current predicament, it is not extreme to suggest that we should allow nature to regenerate native woodlands – our most valuable habitat – across at least a third of the country.[23]

Instead of establishing more conifer plantations, alternative approaches are needed. Mixtures of tree species – managed for timber as well as for water quality, climate and biodiversity in what is known as 'continuous cover forestry' – are one way forward. 'Agroforestry', where trees are part of food production systems, is as old as farming itself. There are many viable methods for expanding Ireland's tree cover in ways that meet multiple objectives.

Temperate Rainforests

The most ecologically exceptional of Ireland's remaining native woodlands are the ancient Atlantic oak woodlands that have managed to survive in parts of the west and south-west. Because the humidity is so high along the Atlantic fringe, these woodlands meet the criteria of a temperate rainforest, where an abundance of moisture-loving mosses, lichens, liverworts and ferns cover every available surface, and are draped across the branches of canopy trees. For thousands of years, temperate rainforests covered much of the west of Ireland. Tall oaks grew together with elm, ash, Scots pine, holly, hazel, rowan, birch and hawthorn, depending on the terrain. Now, because of human activity, only tiny pockets of these Irish rainforests survive.

The most extensive area of Ireland's Atlantic oak rainforests is in Killarney National Park in Kerry. Others survive too, including Glengarriff Woods in west Cork, Uragh Woods in Kerry, and Derryclare Woods in Connemara. Frustratingly, each of these remaining temperate rainforests is overgrazed and riddled with invasive rhododendron, preventing natural regeneration, despite being owned by the state and ostensibly protected under national and European law. Ireland's richest ecosystems are literally dying on their feet.

In addition to Atlantic rainforests of oak, Ireland is also home to oceanic hazel woods, another type of rare temperate rainforest that is unique to western Ireland and Scotland, with most of those that remain here occurring in the limestone landscapes of the Burren in County Clare.

For millennia, oceanic hazel woodlands were so abundant that the Irish word for woodland (*coill* or *coille*) comes from the Irish word for hazel (*coll*). These special woodlands, existing nowhere else on earth, are characterised by a low canopy, plenty of light, and a carpet of rich green mosses. Moss grows so thickly that it extends like fluffy green leg warmers up along the many slender shoots of hazel trees. Every golden-hued bole is delicately patterned with lichens. Moisture-loving ferns thrive, adding to the luscious allure of the whole scene.

Oceanic hazel woodlands contain an enormous variety of fungi and lichen species, some growing high up on branches, some on the bark, others weaving their subterranean filaments through the soil. Several types of 'hazel glue fungi' have evolved to 'catch' falling branches that have temporarily snagged, appearing to glue the dead branches to living trees, extracting their goodness before they fall to the ground.

The rarest woodlands of all are yew woodlands, intriguingly

different because yew is one of only three coniferous trees native to Ireland (along with low-growing juniper and majestic Scots pine). Yew woodlands are dark, mossy places, not obviously bustling with layers of life like most other types of native woodland. Yew trees are very slow-growing and so can live to be many hundreds of years old. Near a limestone outcrop in Killarney National Park that hosts the largest wild yew wood in Ireland, there is a particularly ancient yew tree known as the Killarney Yew. It stands dramatically right in the centre of a ruined abbey from the fifteenth century. The tree may be as old as the abbey itself, and perhaps even older, if the tree that now stands there resprouted from a tree felled by the monks. (Yew trees tend to have 'eternal' life, persisting for hundreds of years, and returning to thrive from cut stumps.)

Spending time in some of these special woodlands is an enchanting experience, and a sure way to re-engage ourselves with the wild potential of Ireland. It is a marvel to experience the density and lusciousness of oak and hazel rainforests, and to consider the incredible timespan of yew trees, who are older than we can know. We are allowed a glimpse into how it feels to be immersed in ancient, entangled communities of interconnected organisms. These places offer insight into what we could be nurturing – and be nurtured by – if we allowed nature some space to recover.

Invitations to the Wild Embrace

❦ Find your nearest patch of broadleaved woodland, no matter how small, and visit often.

❦ In March and April, before deciduous trees grow their leafy canopy and when the ground erupts in spring flowers, go to a woodland and identify delicate wood anemone, dog-violet, wood sorrel, wild garlic, bluebell and primrose.

❦ Listen out for the loud screech of acorn-eating jays in a native woodland.

❦ Visit a temperate rainforest along the Atlantic seaboard and be wowed by the abundance of moisture-loving mosses, lichens, liverworts and ferns draped from every surface. Some Irish rainforests to visit include the oak woods in Glengariff, west Cork; the oak woodlands in Killarney National Park, and the many small pockets of hazel woodland in the Burren, County Clare.

Irish rivers were
manifestations
of female deities

Flowing Water

IN pre-Christian cultures there was a belief that underneath the surface of the earth lay a vast lake. Far more than just a body of water, this lake was the otherworld, the source of all knowledge and wisdom, underlying everything. Its waters surged up as springs, wells, rivers and lakes, making them sacred too, and representing a link between this world and the otherworld. The tradition of holy wells still holds strong in Ireland today.

Since the Bronze Age, people left valuables in springs, wells, lakes and rivers, as votive offerings to the gods and goddesses who inhabited this other realm. Even bogs and marshes were seen as points where the veil between this world and the otherworld was thinnest. Symbolic offerings such as horses' bridle bits, bronze bowls, brooches, bracelets, and hordes of silver and gold were placed in lakes and rivers to show respect for the powerful gods, as offerings of gratitude, or perhaps to appease powerful deities when misfortune had struck, such as plagues or crop failures.

Watery worlds have been held in high regard for millennia. In legends, Irish rivers were considered manifestations of female deities. We know that river goddesses were important right across Celtic parts of Europe. An Indo-European aquatic goddess called Danú is the source of the name for the River Danube. She likely shared the same origin as the Irish goddess Danú, who was mother to a family of mythical warriors, the Tuatha Dé Danann. Sinann was the goddess for whom the River Shannon was named. That female deities were embodied in great rivers reflects a logic that river water brings fertility, and thus is seen as a female force.

Rivers, lakes and wells still have a special draw on us. We go to them for solace, for contemplation or recreation, drawn to the energetic ambience of flowing water. 'Down to the river' is a familiar refrain from songs, poems and hymns across the world, a reflection of the redemptive qualities of water.

In poetry and philosophy, rivers have been taken to represent every aspect of life and death. Rivers begin life as energetic tumbling mountain streams; develop meanders and gather species as they mature; and as they come to the end of their course, broaden out, slow down and deposit their loads before merging with the sea.

A different suite of wild plants and animals have adapted their life cycles and rhythms to the changing pace and flow of the river course, some needing the fast-flowing, oxygen-rich waters of gushing mountain streams, others dependent on the depth and volume of the lower reaches. These are the characteristics to ponder when we next approach a river, as the distinctive scent of water mint wafts up from wet ground underfoot. Curiosity draws us to the river, and we find ourselves wanting to linger longer. It has long been understood that there is wisdom to be had from the water.

Salmon

The bringing of wisdom from the otherworld through natural springs is told in the well-known tale of the 'Salmon of Knowledge'. In this legend, there were nine hazel trees growing by a sacred pool. Some stories locate the pool as the source of the Boyne, others as the source of the Shannon. The hazel trees conveyed great wisdom, on account of where they grew. When salmon ate hazelnuts that dropped into the pool, they acquired the nuts' sacred wisdom, represented as bright spots on the fishes' scales. The wisdom in turn could be passed up to a human who ate the flesh of a salmon of knowledge.

A seer called Finnéces spent many years attempting to catch a salmon of knowledge, eager to acquire the wisdom and poetic inspiration it would impart. When one day he finally caught such a fish, he set it to roast above a fire, watched over by a boy in his care. The salmon began to blister in the flames, and when the young lad burst a blister with his thumb and it hurt, he innocently popped his thumb in his mouth to cool the burn. This boy, whose name was Fionn Mac Cumhaill, acquired all the knowledge and wisdom from the sacred fish, and Finnéces was deprived of that for which he had so long waited. Young Fionn went on to become the leader of the Fianna, a band of hero warriors remembered and celebrated to this day.

It's with good reason that people, down through the ages and across cultures, have been passionately preoccupied with salmon. For their beauty, agility and impressive migration, salmon are worthy of our veneration. Around the world, various species of migratory salmon have been the stars of ancient myths and legends, representing good health, long life and knowledge. It is not uncommon for anglers to travel far and wide for salmon fishing experiences. Researchers have for generations been attempting to decipher the full gamut of the Atlantic salmon's intriguing life cycle and migration. And chefs have developed an infinite number of ways to prepare salmon for the plate.

Born from eggs laid among gravelly pebbles in cool, clean rivers, washed over by well-oxygenated water, often high up in mountain headwaters, young salmon spend up to three years in the river, feeding on aquatic invertebrates, before venturing downriver and out into the Atlantic Ocean. The young fish then swim all the way to the rich feeding grounds of the North Atlantic, sometimes as far as Greenland. When they are ready to spawn, the salmon return to their roots, finding and travelling up the river into which they were born.

How they navigate across open ocean is still poorly understood, a journey that can take over a year to complete, covering distances of 3,000 kilometres. Salmon may somehow use the earth's magnetic field to align their route, a skill we don't yet fully understand.

After its heroic journey, each fish manages to arrive at the coastline at the very mouth of their natal river. Salmon have the ability to smell a droplet of water from their natal stream in the merger of many waters. Detecting remembered smells from the exact branch of the right river, and pheromones from other fish, they know exactly which tributary to swim up. This is where the second, equally impressive leg of their journey commences.

Seeing a salmon leaping acrobatically into the air and swimming upstream against the current is exhilarating, a special thing to behold. From September onward is when salmon mostly travel upriver. A good time to witness this is after a heavy rain when water levels are high. Sadly, salmon leaping is a far less common sight than it was only 50 years ago, when they were so abundant, no one thought the population could dwindle.

Travelling upriver, both male and female salmon are so determined to get to their spawning grounds, they don't eat at all. Instead, they are sustained by the rich fatty flesh they've built up during years at sea. (When salmon snap at a fisherman's artificial fly, they are curious rather than hungry, which I find a little tragic.) Despite not eating, salmon can swim against heavy river currents and leap over rapids and waterfalls several metres high. It's not surprising that ancient legends held salmon in such esteem, and judged a warrior's fitness and acrobatic ability against that of a migrating salmon.

As far back as Mesolithic times, when hunter-gatherers lived here, salmon were being caught in the estuaries of rivers. Five Mesolithic fish traps made of woven hazel rods have been excavated in the estuarine muds near the mouth of the River Liffey. Later Bronze Age traps have been excavated in the Shannon estuary. And woven fish traps have been preserved in tidal muds along the Blackwater estuary, some from the Saxon period from the seventh to the ninth centuries.

We have ample evidence that throughout history, people knew how to work the tides to harvest migrating salmon. After such an iconic history of abundance, it is hard to believe that over just a few decades, since the 1970s, salmon populations have dwindled to such an extent that they are now threatened with extinction in many of our river systems.

The seas salmon travel through are being altered by overfishing and by climate change. Compared to records from 40 years ago, a rapidly diminishing proportion of the Atlantic salmon who go to sea are managing to survive there, and fewer again are completing the return journey. Those that do make it back are finding the rivers in which they were born to be utterly transformed by human activity. Their trips upstream are blocked by dams, weirs, culverts, road crossings and bridge foundations, all of which are barriers to migration. The pools, shallows, eddies and riffles along rivers – all essential salmon habitats – have been scooped away as river channels are dredged to drain off farmland as part of arterial drainage works. The pebbles the fish need to spawn amongst are silted over or scraped away. Half of Ireland's rivers are below the standards required for healthy habitats.[24] River water is polluted by fertiliser run-off and other nutrients, making oxygen levels in the water too low for successful spawning.

Salmon are a key component of aquatic ecosystems. As young fish (called 'fry') living in the upper reaches of rivers, they feed on small invertebrates in the water, whose abundance is determined by the health of the aquatic environment. Small salmon and trout are also an important food for many animals, including kingfishers and otters.

Another animal whose life cycle is enmeshed with that of wild salmon is the freshwater pearl mussel. These are Ireland's longest-living creatures, with a lifespan of 120 years. This means that the oldest living pearl mussels in Irish rivers today were young when the Easter Rising of 1916 and the subsequent Civil War was taking place.

Tiny freshwater pearl mussels, when just starting out in life, overwinter attached to the gills of young salmon and trout, spreading through the river via their hosts' migration. These mussels are now 'functionally extinct' in Irish waters, having been unable to breed successfully for many years because the pristine habitats that they require are no longer so pristine.

Angling groups and river trusts are embarking on the challenge of restoring rivers, with the intention of re-creating healthy habitats for salmon, trout, eel, lamprey and other aquatic animals whose populations have been declining. If we restore our rivers, then at least the salmon who do make it back from their epic Atlantic adventures will be able to spawn again freely; regaining the dignity we have taken from them, and inspiring hope with their admirable strength, wisdom and stamina. Salmon represent a bounty that all rivers rightly deserve.

Mayfly

One of the aquatic insects that salmon and trout like to feed on are mayflies. Mayflies spend most of their lives without wings, living beneath the water, buried in sediments at the bottom of a river or a lake. Each of the 33 species of mayfly that are native in Irish rivers and lakes has its own specific suite of preferences, its own niche in the habitat. After several years as bottom-dwelling nymphs, mayflies reach a time, always at the end of May, when they are finally ready to emerge in the world as delicate and beautiful flying creatures.

To get from the mud to this emergence though, several

steps are necessary, each involving risk. Their hard case fills with gas which helps them float up to the surface of the water. There they pause a while, absorbing the change of scene, the difference in temperature and light, before bursting out of their casings with a brand new set of wings and a long, elegant, three-pronged tail. Hungry trout snatch lots of mayfly at this stage. Fortunately, though, thousands of mayflies emerge together, and their mission is to mate. Each will only live for a few days, a limited spell when the air is thick with mayflies. The space above the water is packed with courting mayfly couples, who in their distracted state are easy prey for swallows, swifts and bats. Mayflies are vital sustenance, just at the time of year when these birds and bats need a good feast of protein to help them fledge their young. Mayflies erupt in such abundance that for thousands of years there has been plenty to go around, and ample eggs are laid to give rise to the next generation, too.

Dipper

Bobbing dippers feast on the caddis flies, stoneflies, mayflies and other invertebrates that also sustain young salmon fry in the river. Dippers are small brown birds with a distinctive white bib who perch on rocks that protrude from fast-flowing water. They bob up and down on the rocks, then dive beneath the current to walk along the riverbed, foraging small insects from in between submerged pebbles.

Because they are such specialists, dippers are vulnerable. They are highly adapted to live by fast-flowing rivers, and rarely wander far from where they were born. If their habitat or the insects they eat are impacted by pollution, or by humans remodelling the river, dippers are left with nowhere to go.

Evolution has made dippers supremely capable of living in a very particular environment. Super strong feet and legs help them cling to the stones as they walk along the riverbed underwater, contending with fast currents just to stay still. These songbirds can walk through swirling eddies of mountain streams, scanning for tiny invertebrates between the stony substrate. To help them see underwater, especially in peaty brown river water, dippers' breasts are covered in white feathers, inbuilt colouring that reflects light from above onto the riverbed, a biologically integrated reflective disk. This clever adaptation helps dippers find enough food to sustain them in such a challenging environment. Their wings are short and sturdy, enabling their underwater manoeuvres, where they push themselves downward to stay submerged in the river current. They also have a large amount of haemoglobin in their blood so they can hold more oxygen, and thus stay submerged for sustained periods without having to come up for air. The Irish name for a dipper is *gabha dubh an uisce*, 'blacksmith of the water', because blacksmiths too would wear aprons across their chests.

Kingfisher

A very different bird to the dipper, but one who also lives along rivers, is the kingfisher. Kingfishers are skilled hunters, able to calculate with precision the speed, depth and velocity of a fish they have their eye on. A kingfisher's dagger-like beak is perfectly evolved for the catch, and it only takes 1.2 seconds to return to its perch with a fish in its beak. These amazing birds can fly as fast as 45 kilometres per hour, so it is rare to get to see one properly. Sometimes they can be seen perched on a branch overhanging a river or stream, watching carefully for fish, though generally, a sighting will be limited to a flash of turquoise and cobalt, a blue blur that is gone before we can even exclaim our excitement.

Listening out for the kingfisher's call – a high-pitched whistle – is one way to help locate them. Recognising the call helps raise the chances of getting a proper view. Because they are territorial birds, and breeding each year takes place in the same stretch of river, getting to know where they are means we can return regularly to watch out for a precious glimpse.

Kingfishers' breeding season gets underway in February and March, so these are good months to try to see them, as they are busily building nests and brooding eggs. Male and female work together to raise their young, bringing a constant supply of small fish back to the nesting hole in the riverbank. One pair can raise as many as three broods each year, but once this work is done, the male stays in the territory, while females take off to a separate but adjacent territory for the winter. Fledglings must leave parental territory and find new places to establish themselves, so autumn is also a good time for looking out for the young, cast-out kingfishers venturing along the river.

The main thing to do if hoping to see a kingfisher, apart from going to a likely stretch of river and being somewhat lucky, is to be still and patient. Kingfishers are hyper-aware of movement in their vicinity, and will avoid an encounter; so be quiet and discreet, so as not to alarm these exceptionally beautiful birds.

Otter

Another expert hunter in rivers and lakes is the otter. I was once perched by a river in December, hoping to catch sight of a salmon leaping up a weir, and instead I saw a scuffle between an otter and a fish, a circular whirling of silver scales with the sleek fur and long tail of an otter. After just a few seconds, the otter clambered ashore with the fish in his mouth, either a salmon or a trout. As it was December the fish had probably spawned, and was exhausted by its epic ocean journey. The otter would likely have been waiting to catch just such a vulnerable fish.

Otters nurse their young for months and train them well in the skills of hunting. They are playful, clever animals. Pups spend about eight months in the family group, playing together as they learn agility, chasing each other in and out of the water, building the strength and sharp wit they will need to survive. Otters are mammals, but their fur is specially adapted to keep them warm, both in and out of the water. Big webbed feet and a long, strong tail make them excellent swimmers and hunters. As well as fish, otters eat a lot of freshwater crayfish (a freshwater crustacean that looks like a little lobster), as well as frogs. Their name in Irish is *madra uisce*, meaning 'water dog'. It's a fitting name for such an intelligent, fun-loving animal; although unlike dogs, otters are very good at not drawing human attention.

Restoration

There is now a welcome upwelling of enthusiasm for river restoration. Excellent manuals exist, community groups are springing into action, and conservation initiatives are expanding. Rivers can be rehabilitated, and the habitats that salmon need can be re-established. As part of this, water quality will have to improve;[25] the current heavy loading of nutrients from fertilisers will have to stop; and the ongoing national dredging programme will have to be drastically reduced. Restoring rivers for salmon can also help improve the habitat for other animals, including stoneflies and mayflies, and all the creatures who depend on them for sustenance.

Before finishing up this look at rivers in Ireland, let's return to the salmon as symbol. The incredible strength and agility of the Atlantic salmon has been inspiring humans here for thousands of years. This extraordinary fish has earned its place in legend as an iconic animal. Like our ancestors before us, we can take inspiration from the salmon for its ability to overcome seemingly insurmountable odds. With sustained effort, recovering the health of Ireland's rivers and lakes is possible.

Invitations to the Wild Embrace

🌱 Check old maps (available online – www.osi.ie) to see if there is a spring or a well near you and visit it.

🌱 From September to November, find a point in a salmon river where you might be able to see them leaping up weirs and cascades. To get the best chance of seeing these impressive acrobatics, go in the early morning or in the evening, when there has been plenty of rain and water levels are up. Some rivers, such as the Moy in Mayo, the Corrib in Galway and the Munster Blackwater, have well-known viewing spots. For other rivers, ask local anglers about locations to see salmon leaping.

🌱 To see a kingfisher, you need a bit of luck. Other factors that might help include going to a likely stretch of river and being still and patient. Catching a glimpse of these exceptionally beautiful birds is worth the wait. Kingfishers are hyper-aware of movement in their vicinity and will avoid an encounter, so you'll need to be ultra-quiet and discreet.

🌱 Find out if there is a river trust in your area and get involved in their restoration actions.

Swallows are a
joy to watch on
summer evenings

Life in the Air

I T'S so normal for us to keep our gaze at eye-level, or to focus downwards, limiting what we see to what's nearby. We rarely look up. When we take a notion to look straight up into the canopy of a tree, it can be like looking at a beautiful painting, filling our field of vision with the fractal patterns of branches, perfect leafy arrangements, and intense shades of green against a blue sky. Because a leafy canopy is an everyday thing, made by nature, we don't give it the acclaim we would if looking at a beautiful painting. But much like we admire a masterful work of art, looking up makes our shoulders drop a few inches and recharges our perspective.

Looking up has a particular effect on our mind, whether on the street or in a woodland, park or garden. When our eyes search the distance, our brains are activated in a different way to when we focus on our immediate surrounds. Looking up at the sky, or taking in distant vistas above the horizon, elicits reflective thinking. There is a good reason why those who designed the grand cathedrals and mosques of the world created such spectacular, high-domed ceilings. Drawing our attention upwards, instead of focusing on the space within our reach, literally changes how we think. When our eyes attune to the distance – to the light on the horizon or a bird up in the sky – our minds tend to follow our field of vision. Watching out to the distance leads us to contemplate that which is beyond our immediate reach, both in time and space. As a result, we think 'bigger' thoughts.

What better way to divert our attention upward than looking up to the sky. When I'm in Dublin, I often hear the sound of geese passing overhead. I made a decision that whenever I hear them, I will immediately put down whatever I'm doing and go outside to look. Craning my neck back, turning my eyes up to the sky, and watching the geese flying across the city in their amazing V formation somehow changes the rest of the day.

Migrations

I became curious to know where the geese flying overhead came from. How do they know how to get here, and why do they always fly in such perfect V-shaped formations?

The brent geese we can sometimes see in Dublin have flown 3,000 miles from Arctic Canada, to spend the winter feeding on eelgrass and algae at low tide in Dublin Bay and other estuaries all around the coast.

During high tide, when their food source is submerged,

brent geese come inland to spend a few hours roosting in open parkland. It is on these journeys that they pass over the city, honking loudly like a reminder for us to look up, like a call to a feathered Angelus.

Other geese we might see passing overhead in winter, including Greenland white-fronted geese, barnacle geese, pink-footed geese and graylag geese, travel from far flung northern breeding grounds in northern Scandinavia, Iceland and Greenland, as well as Arctic Canada, to overwinter in Ireland. Almost half of the world's population of Greenland white-fronted geese spend the winter in Ireland, mostly in the wet fields of the Wexford Slobs.

Flying in a V-shape formation, where one bird leads and the others hold position diagonally to each side, is a collective approach to energy saving. The lead goose takes the brunt of the wind, while each goose that follows travels in the slipstream just behind the wingtip of the goose in front. They take turns flying up front, equally sharing out the time spent in this more demanding position.

Watching these big, heavy birds, knowing they have travelled so far, is truly awe-inspiring. How they navigate is still somewhat of a mystery. Most migrating birds, as well as migrating mammals, have in their noses a substance called magnetite – a magnetically sensitive, naturally occurring mineral that assists animals to detect the earth's magnetic field. Almost like an inbuilt biological compass, migrating animals can orient themselves north-south, as well as determine their east-west position based on the dip of the earth's magnetic field as they migrate from the poles to the equator, or vice versa.[26]

There are still unknowns about how magnetite works and many phenomena that it can't explain. The presence of magnetite, for example, does not explain how animals know exactly where they are, or the geographical reference for where they are going. This skill requires that animals have a mental map, as well as a very good memory for where they have been and where to go next.

Many birds recognise and navigate by landmarks, but this doesn't explain how they cross oceans. It seems that many migratory animals have a mysterious ability to know where they are compared to where they're going; in other words, they maintain mindbogglingly accurate and constantly updating mental maps.

Terns

While geese come here to spend the winter, other birds come to spend the summer months. Terns are elegant little seabirds who weigh less than 100 grams. They arrive each spring to breed in locations around the coast, the only time these masters of migration settle in one place for a spell. They have brains about the size of a pea yet are able to navigate the globe using the polarised light of the sun and the position of the stars. Arctic terns make the longest migrations of any bird, flying almost the full length of the globe, year after year, breeding in the Arctic Circle, then flying to the seas south of South Africa to spend a second summer there.

Terns see more daylight than any other animal, and can feed, sleep and mate at sea. Surviving on a diet of small fish, they can vary their route according to weather and make epic detours when small fish are plentiful elsewhere, nipping across to the Indian Ocean, for example, en route from South Africa to Ireland. The majority of Arctic terns breed in the Arctic Circle, though Ireland is the most southerly breeding place of their range. They once bred all around the coast here, especially in Donegal, Mayo, Galway and Kerry, though not since the twentieth century.

Another tern species, little terns, nest on the beach at Kilcoole in County Wicklow. Their eggs are impeccably camouflaged against the grey pebbles on the shore. Roseate terns breed on Rockabill Island just a few miles off the coast of Skerries in north County Dublin, then fly all the way to West Africa for the winter. Repeating this migration every year for the 10 to 20 years that they live, these beautifully elegant little seabirds clock up serious mileage in their lifetimes. A summer evening stroll along the South Wall in Dublin to Poolbeg Lighthouse is always adorned with the speedy glide of delicate-looking terns, and they are hard to miss on a summer evening by the coast in Dún Laoghaire too.

Terns have stunning courtship rituals, performing a

beautifully choreographed aerial ballet. In the early days of courtship, a pair will fly high together, ascending sharply in spirals, then cross over and zig-zag downwards together again. The dance consists of a continually repeated, carefully coordinated set pattern, as the courting couple assess each other's speed and agility.

There is another element to this that we cannot see. Birds, like many insects, can see ultraviolet light, and freshly grown feathers reflect these wavelengths well. As they dance in close proximity, the birds can admire the flashing bright colours in each other's feathers that are roused by the speed of the wind as they spiral downward. For terns, the romance of the courtship never wanes. Paired terns remain monogamous for as long as they both live, which can be for up to 20 years.

Terns were once widespread around our coastline. In the nineteenth century, they were known as 'sea swallows' for their elegant, streaming feathers. These feathers were admired to such an extent that terns were hunted for fashion, their feathers becoming popular adornments on ladies' hats in Victorian times. The unfortunate result was that most of their breeding colonies in Ireland were obliterated.

By the 1990s, terns' numbers were dangerously low. Conservation projects were initiated by BirdWatch Ireland and others to protect some breeding colonies from predators. When a population is down to a few hundred breeding pairs, predation by rats and gulls can easily be the final nail in the species' coffin. To avert this, each summer specialist wardens guard breeding colonies of terns around the clock, keeping predators away from eggs and greatly elevating the odds of breeding success. This approach has been working wonderfully, and thankfully tern populations have been making a promising recovery.

Now, evening strolls along the Dublin coastline are sure to be accompanied by the sight of terns speeding by, drawing our attention overhead and into the distance, expanding our perception of space and time.

Swallows

Every year in May, when the swallows reappear, I find their return and their effusive energy both uplifting and reassuring. Hundreds of thousands come back to their bowl-shaped nests in outbuildings, barns and old sheds across Ireland. Mostly they return to the same nest they were in last year, although sometimes they make new nests. A defining characteristic of summer, swallows are a joy to watch each evening, gliding gracefully overhead, filling the air with their calls, expertly scooping up thousands of midges and other flying insects as they go.

The graceful flight of swallows was described in that epic of Irish mythology, Táin Bó Cúailnge, when the movement of the hero Cúchulainn's chariot was compared to the gliding grace of the swallow. Early Christian monks wrote effusively about swallows in flight, as do modern-day poets. Each year in March and April, swallows' arrival back from southern Africa is a testament to grace and perseverance. House martins and swifts also complete epic migrations from Africa to nest in our barns and sheds each summer.

Since the start of written history, people have speculated about where swallows disappear to each winter. No one knew how they vanished so abruptly at the end of each summer, only to reappear and pop right back into their same old nests again each spring. Various theories were proposed to explain the mystery. Some believed that swallows spent each winter hibernating at the bottom of lakes. One well-respected English naturalist declared in the 1680s that swallows spent each winter on the moon, and many people believed this.

We now know that the swallows we see arriving in spring have spent a month or more flying 300 kilometres per day to get here. Weighing in at about 20 grammes, swallows navigate using a combination of triangulation by the dip of the earth's magnetic field, polarised light from the sun, and an uncanny knowledge of the entire 9,000 kilometres of their route, flying over the Sahara Desert, the Mediterranean Sea and the many mountains and plains of Europe. They must also be able to keep track of time and distance, and know how to observe and distinguish their surrounds. In short, we do not understand exactly how these birds get here each spring and fly back to Africa each autumn.

We do know that the reason swallows come this far is to avail of our long daylight hours and the plentiful pickings of small flying insects, perfect protein-rich sustenance with which to feed their broods of nestlings. Given their dependence on this food, one of the reasons that swallow populations are plummeting here and across much of their range is the decline in flying insects brought on by our activities.

Flying Without Feathers

Bats have evolved to avail of the night shift in insect-eating, taking over when swifts, swallows and house martins bed down during darkness. Bats are mammals who have evolved the ability to fly, just so they can chase after all the winged insects in the sky. These furry creatures are generally unaware of what it might be like to be bound by gravity to the ground. Watching bats overhead as dusk descends is one of my favourite things: looking up to see the silhouette of their staccato movements as they manoeuvre expertly around trees, seeing with sound, pursuing the many midges, moths and craneflies that are flapping about on summer evenings.

Some butterflies are strong fliers, despite their sometimes clumsy-looking gait. They can even cover impressive distances, though from our vantage point on the ground, we are not privy to their presence high up in the air.

The migrations of monarch butterflies in America are well known. These intergenerational journeys stretch from the northern United States and Canada all the way to California and Mexico for winter. Less well known is that there are impressive butterfly migrations to Ireland, too.

The red admiral – a big, striking butterfly with orange-and-black-patterned upper wings – flies here all the way from southern Europe and North Africa each May and June to breed in our Irish nettles. How a butterfly with a wingspan of 7 centimetres can perform such a feat is a bit of a mystery.

Rather than fly here and back again, the migration is intergenerational, as with monarch butterflies in America. Red admirals who arrive here from sunny southern climates lay their eggs in nettles. The generation that hatch here – feeding on nettles under a homemade tent of nettle leaves spun together with silken thread – emerge as butterflies and spend the rest of the summer drinking nectar from flowers, as well as sucking on the sweet sap from trees and the juice of overripe blackberries. Come September, it is these red admirals – born and reared in Ireland – that can be seen departing from the coast, taking off on their journey towards the south-east, somehow finding their way back to their winter homelands around the Mediterranean.

Invitations to the Wild Embrace

✝ Join a guided group to experience the surprising loudness of the dawn chorus as darkness dissipates.

✝ Learn to identify a few of our most distinctive and familiar birds' calls. Great tits have a repetitive, easily recognisable two-note song; starlings have an impressive range of distinctive whistles, crackling notes and squawks; and the robin's song is delicate and warbling with a repeated 'tic' sound. Song-thrushes have one of the easiest calls to identify because they repeat each short phrase up to three times before moving on to a different phrase. The blackbird's melodious song is one of most beautiful of all this island's birds.

✝ Go see overwintering geese feeding on coastal mudflats at low tide in one of the estuaries all around the country. The geese have flown thousands of miles from Iceland, Greenland and even Arctic Canada to spend the winter here.

🦃 Learn and listen out for the distinctive call of the curlew. While the population of resident breeding curlews has plummeted in recent years, overwintering curlews from more northerly latitudes can be heard all along our coast from August onwards.

🦃 Starling murmurations occur in known locations through the winter months. Find out where there is one in your county, arrive just before dusk, and look up as thousands of starlings gather before joining together to make a swooping cloud of breath-taking synchronised flight, expanding and swirling in wondrous shapes.

Leatherback
turtles travel to
Ireland to feast
on jellyfish

The Big Blue

ALKING along the shore, the sensation of gently breaking Atlantic waves splashing around the ankles is refreshing. Soft, frothy saltwater spilling from the sea onto the shore tickles the skin, imbuing the energy of the ocean, anchoring us into presence. Expansive skies and changing light on the water draw our gaze out over deep and powerful currents. The appearance and dissipation of white wave-crests provide fodder for meditation, existing, then dissolving into the expanse, like thoughts we can learn to let go of.

When we look out to sea, contemplating the surface of the water and thinking 'that is the sea', we are fooled by our perception. The shimmering expanse of greyish-green and blue is a deceptive foil. In truth, there are multiple other realms beneath the waves. Beds of seagrass and forest-like stands of kelp sway in the current, sheltering shoals of mackerel and stunningly patterned wrasse, cryptically camouflaged winged rays, shimmering shoals of sand eels, and rust-coloured crabs scuttling sideways along the sandy substrate. Even when we swim in the sea, we aren't seeing these underwater worlds.

But there are ways to get to know a little of the life beneath the surface. Beachcombing can reveal intriguing bits and bobs: mermaids' purses, delicate sea urchin skeletons, and shimmering oyster shells. Snorkelling provides an additional window; we might see iridescent blue-rayed limpets on kelp at eye level; be captivated by the graceful movements of jellyfish; and watch tiny sea gooseberries like feather-light ballerinas. Scuba diving opens up real wonders. Going out in a kayak or a boat offers opportunities to observe underwater animals when they breach the barrier between our airy world and their salty domain.

Beachcombing

Beachcombing is a wonderfully absorbing activity. Tuning into the colours and textures of the shore, sharpening our vision, occasionally coming across a fragment that reveals some of the wondrous world beneath the waves – these practices offer insights into the creatures to which we are normally denied access.

Finding a mermaid's purse is always intriguing. I love yielding to the childlike curiosity that these strange little objects engender. Mermaids' purses are easy to recognise; they look just like what you might imagine a miniature mermaid's knapsack to look like. They are leathery little pods, with curly tendrils or smooth straps coming from each of their four corners. Some purses are only several centimetres long, others bigger than the palm of your hand. Some are pale yellow, others dark brown and purple. Mermaids evidently come in all shapes and sizes!

Mermaids' purses are in fact the rubbery egg cases of sharks, skates and rays. Their purpose is to protect the developing embryo inside. When the mother creates these little sacs, she attaches them to something anchored to the seafloor, such as seaweed or a rock. After several months, a baby shark, ray or skate will emerge into the shelter of the seaweeds. Finding a mermaid's purse on the shore means that there are probably important fish nursery habitats offshore, sheltering all manner of infant marine creatures from currents and predators.

The little skates and rays who emerge from the purses are flat fish with big, outstretched wings and funny little faces on their undersides. They glide about with enchanting grace in the deep ocean. Skates and rays are incredible creatures, having evolved additional senses to live successfully in the deep sea. Along with sharks, who they are closely related to, they can detect electrical signals, a biological trait known as electroreception. This means that a skate, ray or shark hunting for their dinner can detect the electrical pulse from another creature's heartbeat without seeing, hearing or smelling the creature. Some species can sense a heartbeat from miles away.

There are about 18 species of skates and rays living in Irish waters. Some live only in deeper water, some spend their time nearer the shore. I was astonished to discover that there are also up to 23 species of shark regularly occurring in the seas around Ireland. Not all rays, skates and sharks lay their eggs in mermaids' purses; many give birth to live young.

Next time you come across a mermaid's purse along the shore, recall that this little capsule was once home to a tiny creature that's likely out there now, tuning into the electrical pulses of other creatures' heartbeats.

Oysters

Finding fragments of shimmering oyster shell washed up on the shore is another clue to what's out there beneath the waves. Oyster shells' pearly, silvery white insides reflect the sun's rays on a bright day on the shore. Each shell takes years to grow, as the oyster inside filters out minerals from the seawater and slowly build up their shell, layer by layer. Native oysters, small and slow-growing as they are, build up offshore reefs that can stretch across the seabed for many hectares and contain millions of oysters. The reefs, made from an accumulation of dead oyster shells and living oysters, are home to dozens of other creatures, including seaweeds, sea anemones, barnacles, tube worms, sea sponges, winkles, whelks and starfish. Oyster reefs provide the physical basis for underwater webs of life, and act as nurseries for young fish who need shelter from currents and predators, ensuring bounty among the many layers of underwater ecosystems.

Oyster reefs have mostly been destroyed in the Irish Sea, dredged up in the nineteenth century to feed the enormous appetite for oysters in Ireland and England. Now that native oysters are too few and far between to be able to support harvesting, another species from another ocean is farmed here instead. 'Pacific oysters' can be seen growing on trellises all around the western shores. Plans are afoot to restore natural oyster beds in the Irish Sea, inspired by the success of oyster reef restoration projects all over the world. Because oysters punch way above their weight in providing the conditions for a bountiful sea, restoring native oyster reefs would have significant positive effects on marine ecosystems. Next time you see an old oyster shell on the shore, let it be a reminder that oysters are ecosystem engineers, providing habitat for many other species and offering huge potential for the restoration of marine habitats.

Jellyfish

I find jellyfish enchanting to watch when out snorkelling; their pulsating movement is delicate and mesmerising. The jellyfish we most often find in Irish waters and washed up on beaches are moon jellies, with a pattern of four purple rings in their translucent round bodies. These tiny sea dancers have been swimming about in the ocean for at least

500 million years, longer than most of the lifeforms in the world today.

Because they can sting, jellyfish provoke alarmed reactions from swimmers. A survey asked visitors to the seaside what they are most afraid of in the sea. Rather than big waves, nasty pollution or sharks, the thing that inspires most fear is jellyfish.

I've been stung by compass jellyfish several times. These beautifully patterned creatures, with radial brown lines emanating from their centres, are one of the most common jellyfish in Irish waters. While their sting is unpleasant, it's no more painful than a nettle sting. Other jellyfish – including the mauve stinger and the lion's mane – can cause a more painful sting, but fortunately these species are not so common. Wearing a wetsuit when snorkelling helps protect against stings.

The reason why jellyfish have stinging cells is to protect themselves from predators, and to stun and capture other small animals to eat. The stinging cells of jellyfish are an incredibly intricate and complex mechanism, described as the most complicated single cell found in any animal. The cell is like a balloon under tension. When it comes into contact with a fish or any other object, the balloon bursts and releases a tiny harpoon laden with venom. Human skin is generally too thick for these harpoons to penetrate. For common species like the moon jellyfish, even if the tiny sting manages to penetrate the thickness of our skin, the tingle is not particularly painful.

Moon jellies have a remarkable life cycle. They start out as tiny white translucent polyps attached to the seafloor. These polyps clone themselves, producing a stack of jelly-like disks. Each minuscule disk clone eventually floats away, then grows into an umbrella-shaped jellyfish. When each of these is mature and ready to reproduce, the offspring is not another jellyfish, as such, but instead, a polyp. The dual life cycle starts over again, the polyp attaching itself to the seafloor, in time popping out a pile of new jellyfish.

A recently discovered 'immortal' species of jellyfish has double copies of its genes that repair damaged DNA. It can choose to regress back into a polyp, a reverse metamorphosis, then reattach itself to the seafloor, and begin the cloning process again. This would be akin to us having the ability to melt our bodies down and produce clones of ourselves, each of which would grow into an adult again, thus enabling us to skirt death indefinitely.

Many people are surprised to hear that leatherback turtles travel to Ireland to feast on jellyfish. These huge turtles weigh up to a tonne, and measure as much as two metres in length. In spring, they lay their eggs on sandy beaches along Atlantic coasts of West Africa and the Caribbean, then swim all the way here for the summer months. As many as 400 leatherbacks are thought to be swimming about in Irish waters on any given summer's day, gobbling up mountains of jellyfish. Because jellyfish consist mostly of water, leatherback turtles must

eat over half their own bodyweight in jellyfish every day –
hundreds of kilos – just to get basic sustenance.

Seals

Being watched by a seal is a memorable experience. Its big
dark eyes observe us with curiosity and intelligence. Seals'
whiskered faces are not unlike ours, their expressions non-
chalantly endearing. It's not surprising that coastal communities have retained legends about beings who could switch
between human and seal form, known as 'selkies'. Folk stories
about selkies echo an understanding of how similar seals are
to us.

As mammals, seals suckle their young. From September to
December, grey seal mothers haul themselves up onto remote
beaches in undisturbed areas all around the west coast to give
birth to a single pup each. Seal pups are big, white and fluffy,
and are nursed on a diet of milk that contains as much as 50
per cent fat, giving them the calories to gain weight quickly
so that they might survive the wintry waters of the Atlantic
Ocean. After a few weeks, the seal pups are left to fend for
themselves, quickly becoming agile in the water, learning to
catch crabs, eels, squid and fish.

While the mothers are gathered on isolated beaches minding
their young in winter, grey seal males mate with each of the
females in their harems. Females can delay the development
of the embryo for up to 100 days, giving themselves a chance

to recuperate, after all the effort of birthing and nursing their pups, before becoming pregnant again.

Once they are strong, grey seals swim far and wide, but return to their natal beaches to reproduce. They journey from the Blasket Islands in Kerry to north Mayo and back again, tour further up to Scotland and back, and even travel on occasion to the Faroe Islands out in the North Atlantic. Next time you see a seal watching you from the rocks or a sandy shore, leave them well alone. They may need the space to rest after returning from an exceptionally long journey.

Harbour seals, on the other hand, tend to stay close to their territories. These are the seals you are more likely to see in harbours and swim sites. Unafraid of their human cousins, they occasionally show a propensity to toggle with divers' fins for fun.

Sunfish

Being out in a boat is a fabulous way to experience the expanse of the sea. Sometimes I've noticed a fin protruding from the water, lazily flipping from side to side. Too slow and floppy to be a dolphin or a whale, a fin like this can only belong to a sunfish, the largest bony fish in the world. Sunfish spend about a quarter of their time near the surface, moving their big round bodies slowly through the water, so it's not unusual to see them. They eat enormous quantities of jellyfish every day, along with small fish and fish larvae.

Without much of a head or a tail, sunfish are big, strange-looking circular splodges. Some say they look like giant millstones, earning them the scientific name *Mola mola*, which means millstone. These enormous endearing creatures, who can be seen placidly bobbing about near the surface of the sea, are becoming more common in Irish waters in recent years; their presence, however, is a sign of warming oceans and overfishing. With fewer fish in the sea, there are more jellyfish around. Warmer seas suit both jellyfish and sunfish, so both are becoming more abundant in Irish waters.

Planktonic Oceans

Plankton are tiny ocean organisms that we generally cannot see with the naked eye, although every time we look out to sea we are looking at plankton. It is photosynthesising phytoplankton that give the sea its gorgeous green hues, the colour we know as aquamarine. Because Ireland is perched out near the edge of the continental shelf, our offshore waters are particularly rich in plankton.

Plankton may be small, but they are far from unimportant. Phytoplankton do the job that plants do on land: photosynthesising, taking in carbon dioxide and releasing oxygen, producing about half of the oxygen we breathe.

Phytoplankton play a significant role in many of the major systems that regulate the earth. They draw down or 'sequester' billions of tonnes of carbon dioxide from the atmosphere into the oceans each year. When plankton die, particles of carbon sink from the surface to the deep ocean. In this way, phytoplankton remove about half of the carbon dioxide produced by the burning of fossil fuels; a larger proportion than that consumed by the world's rainforests and all the other terrestrial systems combined.

This ocean sink is in jeopardy, however. As the oceans warm and there is less vertical mixing of cold and warm layers of water, phytoplankton levels have declined by 40 per cent since 1950, and the whole system is out of kilter.

Planktonic creatures also form the basis of the marine food chains. Those who eat plankton directly include mussels, crabs, mackerel, herring and even basking sharks. But plankton are more than just fodder, and neither are they passive organisms. Some plankton produce a compound called dimethyl sulphide (DMS) when they are under attack, preyed upon by shoals of mackerel, for example. This acts as a defence mechanism, as some seabirds are able to detect DMS, including fulmars, shearwaters and petrels. They respond by coming in and eating up the fish. The plankton are using chemical signals to call in reinforcements.

Surprisingly, many whales, the largest creatures on earth, also eat plankton. Several species that pass through Irish waters – namely blue whales, humpback whales, fin whales and minke whales – filter enormous quantities of seawater through a comb-like structure called a 'baleen' in their mouths, extracting planktonic creatures ('zooplankton') and phytoplankton. I love the fact that the largest known animals ever to have existed, blue whales, feed themselves on microscopic plankton.

Ireland is one of the best places in Europe to go whale watching. In late summer and autumn, humpback whales can sometimes be seen off the south-west coast, passing surprisingly near the shore as they make their epic migration from their summer feeding grounds in the polar regions to warmer waters near the equator for breeding and birthing. Enormous fin whales also arrive in Irish waters in late summer.

The relationship between whales and plankton plays a huge part in the carbon cycle and regulation of the global climate. Whales feed at depth, then release their faecal plumes nearer the ocean surface. Out in the open oceans where a lack of nutrients can limit plankton growth, this whale poo is a phytoplankton fertiliser. Enabling so much more plankton to grow allows more carbon to be sequestered by the photosynthesising plankton, and when they die, huge quantities of these plankton sink deep to the ocean floor where they remain for a very long time. This results in a net loss of carbon from the atmosphere to the ocean floor.

As the carbon concentrations in our atmosphere soar to levels higher than ever experienced in the history of humankind, this relationship between whales and plankton is a component of the earth's ecosystems that is working very much in our favour. The more whales there are, the more plankton there is; and more plankton means less carbon in the atmosphere. Allowing whales to recover helps the whole ocean ecosystem to recover. This process makes a significant contribution to the global carbon cycle and to climate change mitigation.

Another way that whales impact the health of oceans is that they are thought to encourage more fish in the sea. Plankton nourished and increased by faecal plumes in turn boost fish populations, so plentiful populations of whales in the sea are thought to be creating the conditions in which more fish can thrive.

When whales were hunted to near extinction in the nineteenth and early twentieth centuries, it was never imagined that they had such an enormous role in the levels of carbon and oxygen in the atmosphere. Fortunately, whale populations are making an impressive recovery from those extreme levels of hunting. They may have an important contribution to make in helping buffer marine ecosystems from destabilising stresses such as overfishing, rising temperatures and ocean acidification.

Marine Protected Areas

One of the ways we can help the populations of whales and other marine life to recover is through protected areas out at sea, called Marine Protected Areas (MPAs). These implement protections for kelp beds, fish nurseries, shark breeding areas, mammal migration routes, highly sensitive cold water coral reefs and other marine habitats, giving sea life some respite from our relentless exploitation. MPAs allow ocean creatures great and small the chance to live out their lives and reproduce in their own unique and wonderful ways, a necessary conservation measure if we wish for amazing species, such as rays and skates, to survive the next few critical decades.

There are lifeforms in the ocean that are more wondrous than we could ever have imagined; creatures only being discovered, whose life strategies defy all expectations. But marine life is more than the sum of its parts. We are now beginning to understand that ocean ecosystems sustain the entirety of life on earth.

Invitations to the Wild Embrace

❦ Ireland is one of the best places in Europe to go whale watching. Seeing one of the largest creatures on earth at close proximity is an exhilarating experience. As well as the occasional glimpse of the dorsal fin of a whale, it's not uncommon to see pods of dolphins whirling about near the boat, circling and pursuing one another at impressive speed. There are many tour boat operators across the country, notably in Cork, Kerry and Clare.

❦ Snorkelling is a great way to see kelp beds full of life, crabs scurrying along the seafloor, and enchanting, ethereal jellyfish moving through the water.

❦ When at the seaside, get absorbed in beachcombing. Look out for mermaids' purses, oyster shells and other evidence of what lies beneath the ocean waves.

'No-mow May'
is a great way to
start the summer

Urban Nature

UNDERSTANDING how biodiversity relates to human health is a developing frontier for science, policy and practice. Every day, neuroscientists and psychologists are making new discoveries about how being in nature, including nature in urban environments, is crucial for the healthy functioning of our nervous system, immune system, stress responses, attention span, problem-solving abilities and capacity for empathy. With a higher proportion of people living in urban environments than ever before, we must get better at bringing elements of wild nature back into towns and cities, so that city dwellers can avail of avail of nature's health benefits.

We know how good it is, for example, to let the kids climb a tree in the local park; to pause and watch a heron perching elegantly by a canal bank; or to glimpse a local fox make her way down the middle of the street at dusk. But imagine urban areas permeated with pockets of native trees, offering shade on hot days and the play of leaf-dappled light and colour through the seasons. Imagine towns where healthy, restored rivers are clean and bursting with an abundance of wild fish, kingfishers, otters, damselflies and more. Where flower-rich habitats are abundant too, butterflies, wild birds and the fractal patterns of ferns can be at least as prevalent as concrete and metal.

When the Covid 19 pandemic had us venturing no more than a few kilometres from home, the cessation of traffic noise allowed us, for the first time, to appreciate just how much birdsong there is in urban areas. Without the constant background noise of cars, trucks, motorbikes and buses, we could hear the singing of blackbirds, wrens, thrushes, sparrows and even migratory birds such as swifts, swallows and geese.

Without such busy schedules and the rush of traffic, we paused longer to chat to neighbours. Cycling in the city was a joy without the subtle, constant stress of car noise and fumes, beeping horns and impatient drivers. We came to a new appreciation of municipal spaces: parks, public squares, wide pavements, quaysides and simple street corners became places where people and nature could coexist.

In a poll carried out for the Irish Environmental Protection Agency, 84 per cent of those polled said that access to nature was important for their physical and mental health.[27] Yet wild places in Irish urban areas are few and far between. There is a notable dearth of street trees in the inner city, even though this is where they are especially needed. Inner city communities are especially denuded of biodiversity, depriving residents of the benefits of nature for physical and mental health. We have allowed a stark inequality to develop in terms of access to natural environments.

Rather than just accepting that this is the way of things, imagine how much better our towns and cities could be. As an exercise, think about your neighbourhood as a place where people and nature have at least as much right to space as concrete, tarmac and cars. Think of the transformation of so many paved areas into winding linear nature trails, where pathways for bicycles, buggies, scooters and skateboards weave their way through the colours and texture of birch, rowan, hazel and hawthorn trees, through which mingle richly scented native honeysuckle and wild rose clambering through.

Urban Trees

Trees in urban settings provide us with opportunities to smell their blossom; watch sunlight glisten on their wet leaves after a downpour; listen to birds singing from their branches; and be calmed by their soothing movements. Trees also filter particulate matter from the air, creating healthy compounds for us to breathe instead, and they fill the atmosphere with oxygen. With air pollution now causing more deaths than smoking,[28] reducing the sources of this pollution and re-foliating urban environments with native trees makes sense.

Urban environments infused with trees and other natural features would not only be good for our health and well-being, but could also do much to enhance resilience to the impacts of climate change, including heatwaves, air pollution, droughts, storms and floods.

A pocket of native trees provides habitat for birds, who bring joy and reassurance to their human neighbours on a daily basis. Patches of native trees also act as stepping stones for the movement and dispersal of wild bees and other urban-adapted wildlife. Hawthorn, crab apple, rowan, bird cherry, willow and hazel are all well suited for pockets of urban planting. Their flowers provide pollen and nectar for wild bees, colourful butterflies, hoverflies, delicately patterned night-flying moths, who in turn support bats, swifts, swallows, blue tits, robins and all the rest. The leaves of native green plants and trees feed multitudes of small creatures too, who in turn provide protein-rich sustenance for blue tits, chaffinches, wrens, blackbirds and dozens of other native birds, some of whom are quite particular in their feeding habits.

Non-native broadleaved trees can be beneficial too, though haven't been established in Ireland for long enough to have become as embroiled in the multitude of reciprocal relationships as native species. With biodiversity declining at an unprecedented rate, it is the webs of interdependent relationships between wild native species that need space to recover lost ground.

From Lawns to Meadows

Huge amounts of urban green space are set aside for tidy green lawns in parks, schools, university grounds, civic spaces and the landscaped areas around office blocks and other suburban buildings. It takes a lot of work to maintain a 'good' lawn: keeping the grass neatly mown and free of moss, and in particular ensuring that no such thing as dandelions or daisies burst into blossom. Lawns are where we rigidly stamp out the colours, textures and diversity that nature expresses, instead imposing our own antiquated standards of conformity, straight lines and sharp edges.

Many acres of green space in urban areas could be brought back to life by allowing wild species to re-establish themselves. Imagine seeing swathes of oxeye daisy, red clover, blushing yarrow, purple knapweed, dainty cowslips and wild orchids on everyday walks to work, school or the shops. Swaying flower heads would provide movement, colour and texture, drawing our attention to their symmetrical shapes and easing our frazzled nervous systems.

About half of Dublin city is not built upon, and green spaces make up a quarter of the land area. Imagine if most of this was restored from sterile greens to bountiful, buzzing, richly scented colourful habitats, life-giving and sustaining. Many people are now practising no-mow May in their gardens, which is a little like a gently negotiated first step in a peace treaty in our relentless war on nature. Managing open green spaces as 'long meadows',[29] which are only cut once per year at the end of the summer, offers rich resources for wildlife. Often, a surprising medley of wildflowers emerge. Knapweed, for example, produces phenomenal quantities of nectar. Allowing wildflowers like these to establish in gardens, parks, roadside verges, civic spaces and schools is one of the best actions that can be taken for biodiversity in urban environments.

Just a year or two of reduced mowing pressure can see expanses of lawns transformed. Cuttings should be removed – rather than be left strewn about to rot back into the ground – in order to reduce nutrients over time, and thus limit certain 'ruderal' species like docks and nettles, which have a tendency to take over. After a year or two, there will be cheerful greetings from many colourful wildflowers, self-seeding and adapted to the conditions on the site. Insect life will follow: bright spotted ladybirds, shimmering shield bugs, solitary bees, singing grasshoppers, bumblebees and hoverflies, all sustained by the diversity of flowering plants that are given the chance to grow from existing seedbanks in the soil.

Patience over packets is advised, as seeds will make their way in from surrounding areas or from the seed bank in the soil, which is far preferable to scattering bought seed. Grass can be kept at different heights in different areas too, allowing for a mosaic of tall meadow grasses side by side with shorter mown paths and play areas.

Swifts – 'the one who goes with the wind'

Native trees and wild flower-filled green spaces sustain healthy populations of insects, which in turn sustain the sky's most high-performance athletes: swifts. Swifts fly at speeds of up to 140 kilometres per hour. Like all good athletes, swifts require a high-protein diet, which means they need a lot of insects. A pair of breeding swifts rearing a nest of baby birds require about 50 grammes of insects every day. Their name in Irish is *gabhlán gaoithe* – the one who goes with the wind.

Swifts only set down once a year to lay eggs and fledge a brood in the cavities of our buildings. Once the young birds fledge the nest, they remain in flight for three whole years, gliding high on currents of air, navigating all the way to Africa and back, sometimes several times over, without ever landing on their feet. Because of their long, narrow, sickle-shaped wings and their high-pitched calls, swifts are not difficult to see or hear in urban and rural areas. Anyone living in a neighbourhood where these masters of the sky are nesting can consider themselves fortunate. There are now less than half as many swifts flying through the skies over Ireland as there were just 20 years ago.

This alarming decline is due in part to a lack of nesting sites. When wild woodlands were still extensive, swifts would return from Africa each May and make their nests in the hollows of trees. They then adapted to nest in the eaves of tall buildings. This relationship has been working well for centuries. But modern buildings offer fewer opportunities for swifts to nest. Cavities are filled and sealed in such a way that swifts can no longer find suitable nesting holes. The good news is that swifts respond really well when we supply them with specially designed nesting boxes, and readily take up residence where swift-nesting bricks are incorporated into new buildings. In villages, towns and cities all over Ireland, communities have begun putting up swift nest boxes on schools, churches, libraries and other community buildings.

Inviting these incredible little sky dancers back into urban areas is an easy way to restore an element of wild wonder in towns and cities. Encouraging more flying fodder for swifts through the creation of space for insects with long meadows, pockets of trees and fewer pesticides will prevent swifts from disappearing in another 20 years.

Rivers and Canals

Most Irish towns and cities can boast otters playing on riverbanks, though these elusive animals are experts at not being seen by us. There are kingfishers nesting in the banks of the Dodder River in Dublin, and even salmon and trout returning to urban rivers. When river and canal corridors join up with other green corridors, networks of interconnected habitats emerge. These can become highways for hedgehogs, squirrels, mice, foxes and even the ultimate predators – peregrine falcons.

Canals are an especially welcome respite of wild space in urban environments, though are not restricted to urban areas. The Irish network of canals was built in the late 1700s and early 1800s to transport goods around the country. My paternal great-grandfather was a 'lighterman' on the Lagan Canal, captaining a barge transporting coal from the Belfast docks to Lough Neagh, and turf from Lough Neagh back to Belfast. I grew up hearing stories from my dad about summer days on the barge. He loved the wildlife, tow-horses, and fishing for dinner on his canal adventures with his grandad.

Even though they are a man-made rather than a natural feature, canals have been colonised by an impressive range of freshwater wildlife. The water quality of canals here is generally good, as they are protected from the agricultural runoff and other pollution that most of our rivers suffer from. The always slow-moving water soothes our senses and entices us to enjoy unfolding fronds of water lily leaves, colourful dragonflies darting about in pairs, and comically upturned ducks searching for underwater food.

Dividing the tow path from the surrounding land, treelines provide sheltered corridors for bats on their nightly hunting forays. Daubenton's bats in particular hunt for aquatic insects low along the water and are a joy to watch as dusk sets in, speeding along just above the water surface.

Along the canal water's edge grow tall bulrushes, their dark brown sausage-like heads characteristic of canal sides. These heads are made up of hundreds of minute brown flowers which in the summer, when pulled apart, erupt into masses of white fluff, each seed with its own stringy parachute to catch the wind. Thickets of bulrush provide shelter for nesting mallard and moorhen.

Canal sides are home to one of my favourite flowering plants, the tall yellow flag iris, *feileastram* in Irish. Flag iris grows where its feet can stay wet in heavy clay soils. Because the canal banks were constructed with clays, flag iris loves the soggy edges of canals. Its tall architectural leaves are long and spikey, and its flowers are yellow and stunning. These wild irises are related to the iris flowers we grow in our gardens and buy from florists. Gorgeous swathes of cowslips – a flower that used to be common on farm fields but is now relatively rare – also grow along the edge of canal tow-paths in May.

Damselflies and dragonflies skirt among the flag iris, perching as they watch for prey. These feisty but fragile creatures are superb hunters. Their iridescent bodies have distinctive colours and markings, each species with its own unique pattern. Damselflies and dragonflies can be hard to creep up on, because with their enormous eyes covering most of their heads, they can see in almost every direction at once.

Grey wagtails, birds which are in fact yellow with tinges of green and grey, can often be seen along canals, wagging their tails incessantly. They are the ultimate lovebirds, pairing for life, monogamous, and sharing equally the task of raising their young. Extraordinarily graceful and agile as they catch flies mid-air, grey wagtails are well worth watching out for by canal lock gates.

Invitations to the Wild Embrace

🌱 Explore the possibility of erecting swift nest boxes on the side of your home, the local school or community centre, or anywhere with the right set of conditions for swifts. Nesting boxes need to be at least five metres above ground with open airspace for swifts to access the nest in their characteristically high-speed direct flight.

🌱 Look out for grey wagtails around canal lock gates and bridges, where they nest and chase insects over the water during the summer months.

🌱 Contact the parks department or biodiversity officer in your local authority to advocate for more street trees planted near where you live. Planting pockets of native trees in your area, such as birch, rowan, hazel, crab apple and hawthorn will provide resources for urban wildlife.

Bats 'see' in
the dark by
using sound

Nature at Nighttime

UNLIKE owls, foxes, bats and moths, we humans have evolved to function best during daylight hours. Our eyes are adapted to daylight, so we can become disoriented in darkness, and disinclined to venture out in nature at nighttime. But in a world flooded with artificial light, rediscovering darkness can be a wonderful revelation. Nighttime brings a new perspective. Sight is limited but hearing is heightened. Without the mental clutter of daytime, there can be a greater stillness of mind. We become more porous to the presence of creatures who are active by night, tuning our senses to a scuffle in the undergrowth, a squeak from afar, a scent wafting through the air, or a hint of shifting shadows.

On a moonless night, in total darkness, we don't even see outlines. But when the moon is bright, our vision is hardly compromised at all. The world takes on a monochromatic gleam where only silhouettes prevail.

Each nocturnal ramble begins with letting your eyes adapt to the dark. It takes about 10 minutes for night vision to work at all, and a further 30 minutes to fully adjust to night vision mode. Once your eyes have adapted to darkness, if they are suddenly exposed to bright light, for example from a mobile phone or a torch, a light-sensitive pigment in the eyes bleaches out the ability of night vision and it will take a full 40 minutes to regain. Bringing a torch on nighttime adventures is advisable for safety but try to leave it turned off. It can be helpful to have a head torch with a red light setting, which allows you to see the terrain when you need to without interrupting the eyes' dark-adapted vision. Knowing your route in advance is a big advantage, as is going with someone who is familiar with the path. Go slowly and use all your senses to feel your way.

When we venture out in darkness, we become more reliant on sound to read our surrounds, more able to imagine life from the perspective of a bat, a fox, or an owl. Nocturnal animals have evolved some spectacular adaptations for nocturnal living. Foxes, badgers and hedgehogs are endowed with excellent senses of smell and hearing to help them hunt in darkness, to the point that they can hear beetles and earthworms wriggling about in the ground. In this way, badgers pinpoint their prey before going to the effort of digging in the earth with their powerful claws and poking with their long snouts to catch their dinner. Badgers are especially keen on earthworms, slugs and beetles, which make up the bulk of their diet.

Bats

The threshold of dusk is the ideal opportunity to attune ourselves to the night. When we sit out quietly or stroll slowly, bats are often the first nocturnal animal we see. These gorgeous little creatures are all around, flying in the lee of hedgerows, skimming mayflies and midges from just above the river, swooping low along a line of trees.

We give bats a bad rap, for no good reason. These adorable animals nurse their young with great care, live more than ten years, maintain family connections year on year, and are the only mammals that can fly. Many of us know that bats use echolocation to locate and catch their prey – the midges, moths and crane flies who are flying about at night – but the technicalities of how echolocation works are fascinating, and worth describing further.

'Blind as a bat' is a false metaphor. Bats have good sight, but because it's dark at night, vision is of limited use for catching night-flying insects. Bats' development of unique nocturnal hunting skills, combined with their amazing ability to fly, created an evolutionary opportunity for these winged mammals – their own special niche in the ecosystem.

As they go about their nighttime forays, bats are constantly producing high-frequency sounds which go out in waves, hit off objects and return as echoes. As each bat swoops through its three-dimensional world – up over hedges, down under the branch of a tree, through a gap in the hills and alongside an old building – it is continuously reformulating the incoming data about where it is in relation to everything else; never crashing, constantly calculating the information received through echoed clicks and whistles. Bats can 'see' in the dark by using sound to create a non-stop series of sonic snapshots of their surrounds.

Listening to a bat through a bat detector is an awesome revelation of what's going on around us at night. While watching the winged silhouette flying back and forth, a bat detector allows us to eavesdrop on the percussive pulsating sounds that bats produce as they hunt. The sounds they use to scope out their surrounds are different to the sounds they use in pursuing their insect prey. With a bat detector, the evening's soundscape is transformed into a wondrous realm of strange rhythms.

Each different species of bat has a particular range of echolocation calls, set to detect the frequency of particular flying insects. Brown long-eared bats, for example, feed primarily on moths, so their sound pulses are tuned to a frequency that will collide with a moth. Pipistrelle bats primarily eat midges, so the soundwaves they produce are set to collide with the small size of a midge. This is how we know, when listening to bats through a bat detector, which species we are hearing. Bats are also audible without a bat detector, for younger people especially. As we age, our ability to hear peripheral frequencies deteriorates, although even as an adult, it is not unusual to be able to hear at least some of the strange sounds bats make without a bat detector.

Moths, on the other hand, find their way about through smell, to find the flowers they drink nectar from. Some moths have also evolved ear-like appendages so they can hear the high-frequency sounds with which bats locate them. Knowing when they are being pursued allows these moths to take swift evasive action, dive-bombing downwards, or spiralling about in loops to confuse pursuers. These high-speed chases are taking place each night, out among the trees and hedges, when most of us are tucked away in bed.

All our bat species are protected by law. If you are lucky enough to have a roost in your attic or outbuilding, please don't disturb them.

Owls

Owls are masterful nighttime hunters, beginning their silent search for prey each evening as dusk descends. Owls are often heard, though rarely seen. Their wing feathers are designed to dampen the sound of their flight so as not to alert potential prey of their pending demise. Owls have exceptional hearing, so that even on the darkest of moonless nights, finding food is not a problem for them. Gliding overhead, they listen for rodents squeaking and rustling about on the ground below. Their big faces are shaped like a satellite dish, amplifying the little squeaks and scuffles of a mouse as it scampers about below. Owls' ears are placed asymmetrically on their heads, allowing them to triangulate precisely the location of their prey before swooping down to snatch their fur-covered dinner in their talons with maximum efficiency.

Owls have impressive adaptations for night vision, too. The irises in their eyes can open almost completely, receptive to even the tiniest amount of light. Owls' ability to see in the dark is why we have traditionally associated them with wisdom, when darkness was a metaphor for ignorance. They can see what others cannot.

In Ireland there are two resident owl species: barn owls and long-eared owls. The distinctive 'twhit-twhoo' sound often associated with owls is made by tawny owls, a species that is not present in Ireland.

Young long-eared owls are often audible in summertime. When the young owlets leave their nests, they are still unable to fly or to hunt very well, so they perch themselves somewhere nearby and screech for their parents to come and feed them. The distinctive call sounds like a squeaky old gate, designed to carry over a long distance. Once you are aware of these owlet calls, by listening to the locations of the sounds, you might be lucky enough to see an owl parent swoop silently by, an awesome and unforgettable experience.

Owls were once a lot more common in the countryside, their presence valued because of their appetite for rodents. Old farmyards often had barn owl 'windows' specially built in, to encourage owls to nest there. By catching two dozen rats or more each night, a pair of resident barn owls feeding a brood of owlets would be a very welcome presence around the farm: allies against rodents raiding the grain store. In recent decades, however, as the use of rodenticides has grown, the population of barn owls has drastically declined. These toxins accumulate up the food chain, and predators at the top are inadvertently poisoned. Owl conservation measures in recent years have started to show some success, so there is hope that these majestic creatures will become widespread once again.

Manx Shearwaters

Manx shearwaters spend most of each year out at sea, only coming to shore to nest in colonies on offshore islands. Having adapted so thoroughly to life at sea, these birds can hardly walk on land, making them vulnerable to predators such as gulls. For this reason, they keep themselves hidden away in underground burrows during daylight, and only come and go from their colonies on dark nights.

Each parent takes turns to go out fishing, staying at sea for four or five days at a time, sometimes flying as far as the Bay of Biscay in northern Spain and back again, for just a few days' worth of fish-foraging. On especially dark summer nights, the parent who stayed home with the super fluffy chick makes lots of noise to welcome their partner home to the burrow, bellowing out their loud and eerie 'cackling' call. On moonless nights, when all the adults in a colony are calling, the air is filled with an outrageous cacophony of noise.

Manx shearwaters leave their Irish nest sites in July, travelling across the Atlantic to the coast of South America where they spend the winter.

Bioluminescent Plankton

One of the most magical of all nighttime experiences in Ireland is swimming amongst bioluminescent plankton on summer nights along Atlantic shores. When bioluminescent plankton are out in strength, every movement in the water is twinklingly illuminated. Swimmers' limbs are lit up in phosphorescent light, and each splash throws a thousand tiny shooting stars across the water. When I first experienced phosphorescent plankton, I had never heard of such a thing before, so I was astonished as I ventured into the water. The more I moved about, the more the water sparkled.

I later found out that phosphorescent plankton produce light from an enzyme reaction inside their microscopic bodies when they are mechanically disturbed. It is thought that this evolved as a defence mechanism. When there is a disturbance in their midst – such as a plankton-eating fish – the phosphorescent plankton emit light, known as 'bioluminescence', to draw the attention of predators higher up the food chain, so that the planktons' attacker might itself get taken out. This means that any body – whether it belongs to a fish, a dolphin, or a human swimmer – gets illuminated in blue light if it happens to swim in water at nighttime where there are phosphorescent phytoplankton.

Artificial Light

Nocturnal animals, including insects, fish and mammals, have evolved specific behaviours to take advantage of the darkness of night. Now, however, many areas are impacted by an abundance of artificial lighting. Artificial light at night disrupts our own circadian rhythms,[30] and can also disrupt the behaviour, hormones and hunting abilities of many nocturnal animals. Some species of mayfly, for example, have only a few days to migrate upriver to mate. When they encounter brightly lit bridges, they become disoriented, and can fail to follow their traditional routes and thus fail to mate.

Floodlighting playing pitches and car parks through the night interrupts the flight passage of many moths, bats and owls. Because we illuminate our cities throughout the night, some animals are drawn to the light, become trapped, disoriented and fail to find a mate. Others who navigate by the stars, including Manx shearwaters, are drawn off course and lose their way.

Artificial light at night is one of the impacts on the natural world that is relatively easy to address, requiring that nighttime lights are limited to where and when they are necessary; and that outside lights are capped in order to face downwards rather than lighting up a large area. The colour of light is also important: cool spectrum lighting in blue, violet and ultraviolet wavelengths is more harmful, whereas many species are less sensitive to red, orange and amber light.

The Sky at Night

For most of human history, the night sky was relevant. People referred to the location of the rising and setting sun on the horizon to note the progress of the seasons, and the movement of the constellations overhead to measure the passing of time. People depended on starry skies to navigate at sea. The movements of the cosmos and the phases of the moon informed the best timing to gather wild plants, harvest crops, and hunt for certain prey such as migratory birds and fish.

The night sky seems to have always played a role in people's creation myths, right across the globe. Constellations such as Orion the Great Hunter, Leo the Lion, or Taurus the Bull form the basis of stories, beliefs and ideologies. These bright and readily recognisable patterns move in set cycles through the seasons, so it is not surprising that they played such a significant role in people's lives, providing a sense of dependable order and consistency in what could often seem like a chaotic world.

The glimmering light of the stars overhead still literally frames our world. When stars are visible, we are innately drawn to gaze up, watching their expanse of mesmeric movement.

Stargazing on a dark, clear night can feel transformative.

On a purely physiological level, experiencing the night sky has health benefits. When our eyes detect falling light levels, the pineal gland in our brain releases melatonin. Melatonin is a 'darkness hormone' which helps blood vessels to dilate, helping us to feel tired and ready for rest, and stimulating white blood cells which support our immune systems.

Yet now, with most people unable to see the Milky Way because of artificial light at night, the night sky is largely obscured, and we pay hardly any attention to the celestial sphere. Leaving the city and going to spend time where the night sky is visible is a memorable experience, and there are many places in Ireland where night skies are superb.

Spending time in the remote mountains of the north-west, where the night sky is exceptionally vivid, I have come to deeply appreciate all it has to offer. I love being able to step outside and watch the stars, and I miss being able to see the night sky when spending any length of time in the city. I have learnt to recognise some of the constellations, though I'm generally content just to be awed by the bounty of stars, the wash of the Milky Way, and the contemplation that accompanies a good gaze up into a sky full of stars.

In August, Perseid meteor showers fill the night sky with shooting stars. Some are instantaneous flickers; others have long tails – so exciting to see. Lying back to watch this spectacle each August, in a place where light pollution is minimal, is one of the best ways to appreciate the wonder of the celestial sphere.

Fifty different constellations are visible from Ireland with the unaided eye. In summer, Cygnus the Swan 'flies' through the Milky Way. Vega has a slightly blue tinge and is one of the brightest stars in the sky. Acrylla is the Eagle constellation, and Delphinus is a tiny dolphin-shaped constellation. Ursa Major, also known as the Plough, can be seen all year round.

Locating the Plough in the night sky is how we can find Polaris, the North Star. By following your gaze up from the two stars at the end of the Plough, look for the brightest star all out on its own. This is Polaris, the one constant in the night sky, sitting directly over the North Pole. The measure of its distance from the horizon is how people can calculate how far they are from the North Pole, otherwise known as latitude.

In winter we can look out for Capella by its distinct yellow tinge, the sixth brightest star in the night sky. Capella is actually two stars very close to one another, but they shine together as one point of light. While many stars are millions of light years away, probably no longer in existence, Capella is only 42 light years away, which means that the light we are seeing from Capella began its journey only 42 years ago. By contrast, Andromeda is nearly 2.5 million light years away from us, one of the furthest things that we can see with the naked eye. Its light has taken 2.5 million years to reach us.

When we look at the stars we are literally looking back in time. It's a powerful prompt for contemplating deep time and our place in the universe.

Invitations to the Wild Embrace

🌱 To eavesdrop on bats' echolocation sounds, contact your local bat conservation or wildlife group to join a bat walk guided by experts.

🌱 Get a bat detector for yourself and your family – you'll find it surprisingly entertaining for adults and children alike.

🌱 Listen for juvenile long-eared owls calling out at dusk – their call sounds like a squeaky gate.

🌱 During the summer months, go swimming after dark in waters filled with bioluminescent plankton. Every splash is like a milky way full of little stars. Bioluminescent plankton occur regularly in Lough Hyne, a marine sea lough in West Cork. Kayaking is another great way to experience this phenomenon; every drop of water from the end of the paddle lights up.

🌱 Kerry International Dark Sky Reserve, Mayo Dark Sky Park and OM Dark Sky Park and Observatory in the Sperrin Mountains in Northern Ireland are ideal locations to watch meteor showers and look out for constellations.

The word 'bog'
comes from the
Irish for soft

Bearing Witness

W E are currently living through a very particular time in human history, in which natural habitats are fraying at a rate never seen before. Right here in Ireland, butterflies, wild bees and other insects are declining with alarming speed. Once-abundant eels, who travel all the way here from the Sargasso Sea near the Caribbean and back again to spawn, are critically endangered. Majestic hen harriers are now a rarity in their traditional upland strongholds. The decline of each of these iconic species represents loss of the healthy habitats which they need to survive and thrive. Dozens of native plants and animals that were ubiquitous in the 1970s and '80s are now threatened with extinction on this island.

One of the most well-documented species declines in recent decades is that of the corncrake, which winters in Africa and returns to Irish meadows each summer to breed. The long migration is worth the effort because of the richness of invertebrate life in a bustling Irish meadow in summer, providing essential sustenance for young corncrakes.

Corncrakes are secretive and rarely seen, though their loud, distinctive rasping call was the soundtrack of summer all over rural Ireland until populations plummeted in the 1970s and '80s, mostly as a result of the changing management of hay meadows. There are now about 150 breeding pairs nesting in Ireland each summer, a number so low that the survival of native breeding corncrakes here is in jeopardy.

A similar trajectory is facing the curlew, a bird whose haunting call, well-known silhouette in the sky and long, downward-curving beak were once a staple sight and sound of damp pastures all over Ireland.[31]

Breeding curlews need soft, wet ground that yields to their probing beaks; places where earthworms and insects are plentiful for their hungry chicks. They breed on the moist, spongy bogs of the midlands and peaty uplands, and amid the rushes of damp pastures. Curlews are ground-nesting, so need open ground and a clear view to watch out for predators.

But draining off the water from pasture and bog has left our populations of breeding curlew bereft of the soft ground they need. The march of conifers across the uplands has also taken its toll on their habitats. For curlews, it's been a case of death by a thousand cuts, as 90 per cent of the Irish breeding population has been lost since the 1970s.

There is a constant stream of new additions to the endangered species lists. A multitude of devastating losses are cascading through ecosystems, the demise of one species precipitating the decline of another, as the threads of the entangled web are pulled apart incessantly. Throughout human history, there have been many periods of dramatic change, as described in earlier chapters. The difference between those previous periods of loss and now, however, is the rate at which habitat loss and degradation is currently occurring. Government and industry responses do not reflect an appropriate sense of scale or urgency.

Everything, everywhere, all at once, is being forced to adapt or die.

The good news is that awareness of environmental issues is growing; habitat restoration and conservation projects are achieving successful outcomes; and momentum for change is building. But while positive efforts mount, vast quantities of public money are still being channelled to subsidise powerful and environmentally destructive industries. Each year, governments across the world channel taxpayers' money into the fossil fuel industry, aviation, and subsidies for industrial agriculture and overfishing. Acknowledging, even just to ourselves, the inadequate and even perverse responses from those in power can be maddening.

Witnessing the demise of nature can feel overwhelming, but we must not turn away. The purpose of this book is to encourage you to spend time in nature; rekindling life-affirming relationships with wild plants and animals, cultivating curiosity, and gaining fluency in the many wondrous natural phenomena that we are fortunate enough to still have in Ireland. I hope these pages inspire you to explore the mossy layers of a deciduous woodland in spring, to learn to identify some familiar wildflowers, and to listen out for starlings, swifts and swallows overhead. I am convinced that disconnection between people and nature is at the root of the biodiversity crisis. If we were more connected, more able to recognise how much our culture and our well-being is entwined with nature, we simply wouldn't allow the destruction to continue.

To give a sense of how biodiversity loss in Ireland is gathering pace, I have chosen just three examples of threatened Irish habitats for this chapter: grasslands, peat bogs and the sea.

Grasslands

Hunkering down amid the tall grasses and wildflowers of a summer meadow can be a glorious experience. Tall heads of grasses wave in the breeze, creamy white meadowsweet blossom wafts out its rich scent, and glistening yellow flowers of meadow buttercup sparkle in the sunshine. Once we attune our eyes and ears to life within the sward, we can hear grasshoppers singing loudly and the buzzing wings of wild bees.

We have dozens of different types of 'semi-natural' grasslands across Ireland,[32] each a product of soil type, altitude, location and management, each with its own suite of specialised plants and animals that have adapted over thousands of years. Ireland's semi-natural grasslands rely on human management.

In the case of a meadow, harvesting for hay at the end of each summer maintains its species mix; while for a pasture, grazing cattle or sheep maintain the habitat as a grassland and prevent its natural succession into scrub and woodland.

Rich in a diversity of flowering plants, sedges and many types of grasses, semi-natural grasslands are sustenance for tiny flies; dozens of species of hoverflies and glimmering beetles; intricately patterned butterflies; numerous types of wild bee; web-weaving spiders and night-flying moths. Five different species of grasshopper live in Irish grasslands, each with its own habitat preference and its own loud, distinctive song.

Anthills are a sign that a grassland has been in place for hundreds, or even thousands, of years. They disappear when fertilisers are applied, or when the ground is ploughed and re-seeded. Semi-natural grasslands right across Ireland have now been denuded and replaced with more intensively managed ryegrass fields, or converted to other uses such as plantation forest.

In the absence of fertilisers and pesticides, a network of fungal threads and thousands of soil-dwelling creatures live beneath the ground. An array of wild birds depend on these ecosystems, especially for all the insect life they contain. Insectivorous swifts, swallows and house martins scoop up flying insects. Ground-nesting birds such as corncrake, lapwing, curlew and snipe are completely dependent on open grasslands. But these species-rich semi-natural grassland habitats are fragile. Life in them is easily disrupted. The simple addition of fertiliser favours more competitive types of grass which outcompete sedges and wildflowers, resulting in a dramatic reduction of plant diversity. Ploughing, draining and re-seeding have similar effects.

Recent scientific surveys have revealed an alarming rate of loss of these precious grassland habitats as a result of agricultural intensification since the 1980s.[33] As a result of these sudden and dramatic changes, butterflies dependent on grasslands have also fallen sharply. More than half of Ireland's wild bee species have undergone substantial declines since 1980, and a third are considered threatened with extinction. This latter group mainly comprise bees associated with grassland habitats. Many other insects, for which we have no monitoring data, have been impacted also.

As grassland management becomes more intensive, with success measured only in terms of the quantity of milk produced for export markets, biodiverse grasslands have been replaced with fields that specialise in growing one type of grass: perennial ryegrass. This nutrient-hungry grass grows quickly and provides fodder for grazing cattle. It is now probably the most common plant in Ireland. The erstwhile patchwork of mosaic of green grassy fields, once core to Irish cultural identity, is now a monoculture of perennial ryegrass. The myriad of lifeforms dependent on species-rich grasslands have been quietly disappearing with barely a nod of farewell.

Meanwhile, the ramping up of dairy output, one of the main drivers of these changes in recent years, is heavily subsidised and widely celebrated. Apart from driving biodiversity loss in the fields subject to intensification, the increasing use of nitrogen and phosphorus fertilisers is causing widespread pollution of aquatic ecosystems. Ireland's highly specialised dairy industry is also heavily reliant on imported soy and grains to feed cattle in winter months.[34] This means that in addition to driving down diversity here, the impacts of feed production in source countries such as Brazil have been wreaking ecological havoc in other places too.

Support schemes to maintain farmland habitats have been in place for decades; however, these have been poorly designed and implemented, making them ineffective in their stated objective of halting the decline of farmland biodiversity.[35] This is despite €2.18 billion having been distributed to farmers in Ireland between 1994 and 2006 under environmental schemes as part of the EU Common Agricultural Policy (CAP).[36]

The subsidised annihilation of Ireland's biodiversity is a scandalous use of public money, and a tragic demise of the rich tapestry of life that for millennia has characterised this island's agricultural landscapes. Fortunately, there are many viable solutions which can turn these trends around. These include specific conservation schemes for species-rich grass-land habitats and for threatened birds such as corncrake and curlew.

'Results-based' payment schemes are a novel approach that have demonstrated impressive positive outcomes for threatened farmland biodiversity. Participating landowners are paid according to the habitat quality of each field in the scheme. For these schemes to work as intended, great care must go into their design and implementation.

Peat bogs

Peat bogs are made up mostly of water and infilled with soft, soggy sphagnum mosses, also known as bog moss. The word 'bog' comes from the Irish for soft, like the saying, *tóg go bog é* – take it softly or take it easy. As we discussed earlier, in ancient times bogs were considered sacred places, where water, earth and sky merged, where the veil between this world and the otherworld was thought to be at its thinnest. This same soft wetness is why plant matter in living, active bogs accumulates as peat.

The conditions are so wet and stagnant that there is no oxygen, so normal decay processes are impeded. Nothing breaks down properly in a wet bog. This is why 10,000-year-old tree stumps and the sacrificed bodies of kings from more than 2,000 years ago are so well preserved in Irish peat bogs.

These strange circumstances leave few nutrients available to growing plants, so some have evolved highly specialised ways of overcoming this challenge. Sundew is a small insect-eating plant that grows in Irish peatlands. Sundews have glistening, sticky, red-tipped tentacles which passing insects mistake for a tempting droplet of nectar. Once they land on one of these tentacles, they find themselves stuck. Over the course of a few days, the plant secretes digestive enzymes to consume its insect catch. This is a highly unusual method for a plant to get the nutrition it needs, but these gorgeous little sundews are not difficult to find when you venture out on a healthy midland bog. Butterwort is another type of carnivorous plant that grows on peat bogs; its leaves emerge from watery pools that pattern the surface of raised bogs.[37] Butterworts have gluey leaves with which to catch flies.

Since the loss of Ireland's woodlands, people have turned to peat bogs for fuel. Turf cutting during the summer months became part of Irish culture. In the 1950s, industrial-scale peat mining began in earnest, fuelling electricity generation and providing jobs where they were much needed. Vast tracts of bog have since been drained, harvested and burnt for electricity. Now, less than 50,000 hectares of the original 310,000 hectares of raised bog in Ireland remains relatively intact.

Peat bogs also store vast quantities of carbon which is released when the bog is drained and dries out. Drained peatlands in Ireland are releasing eleven million tonnes of carbon dioxide into the atmosphere each year – the same quantity of carbon dioxide emitted by the energy sector here in 2018.

In the past twenty years, we have become increasingly aware of the climate and ecological consequences of harvesting peatlands for fuel. Yet drainage and harvesting has continued. Bord na Móna continued industrial harvesting until 2022. Mining for horticultural peat moss, used in commercial horticulture and private gardens, is ongoing. In the uplands, peat soils continue to be actively drained, harvested for turf, and planted up with sitka spruce monocultures – despite the well understood climate emissions that arise, and the ecological implications both for the bog itself and for the streams and rivers that receive the eroded peaty particles. Turf-cutting contractors have fought a vicious battle to continue to harvest turf, even on the few remaining bogs that were somewhat ecologically intact and worthy of restoration. All over Ireland, people remain committed to burning turf and peat briquettes in open fires, despite it being more climate-polluting even than coal.

Today, 'active' raised bog covers only 0.6 per cent of their original area. Just a small proportion of the raised bogs worthy of conservation are being actively protected and restored. The state has an atrocious record of failing to implement environmental law that protects peat bogs. Even in the throes of a biodiversity crisis, we cannot agree on practical actions to effectively carry out peatland protection. On the upside, peatland rewetting and rehabilitation is gaining pace in Ireland; it offers a great deal of hope for the future if more widely rolled out.

The community in Abbeyleix, County Laois, when their local bog was about to be industrially harvested by Bord na Móna in the early noughties, decided to act. They protested, resisted and negotiated with the company for the right to protect and restore the bog, rather than let it be harvested. After a long but eventually successful campaign, the bog was spared. Now the 'men's shed' movement has been building wooden walkways so that people can access the bog and enjoy watching wildlife there. Local schools monitor dragonflies and birdlife. Many in the community are involved in blocking drains to restore the peaty habitats. Initiatives like this are now happening all over Ireland, with communities actively participating in the rewetting and restoration of peat bogs.

The sea

The sea is generally beyond what we tend to consider within our realm of influence. It is so vast that we imagined it was too big for us to inflict serious damage. Over the past 60 years, however, scientists have been learning that this is no longer the case.

In Irish waters, thriving kelp beds, cold water coral reefs and other marine habitats are teeming with life, sustaining healthy ecosystems well beyond their actual footprints. Yet just as we are awakening to the wider importance of these underwater worlds, scientists are increasingly expressing concern at the severe damage resulting from our activities.

For example, the 23 species of shark who are at home in Irish ocean territory are slow growing and long lived, making them vulnerable to overfishing. One quarter of the sharks, rays and skates in Irish waters are now threatened. Because most sharks are predators, their presence regulates many other organisms below them in the food chain, maintaining balance in ocean ecosystems. When their population is reduced, the entire web of marine life is impacted.

Cold water reefs were only discovered in the 1990s on Ireland's continental margin. Some are over 100 metres in height and span several kilometres, all bustling with life. Yet as they were being explored, it became evident that some were already half destroyed by bottom trawling for fish.

Kelp beds, cold water reefs and other marine habitats store carbon away from the atmosphere. Just like peat bogs, when we destroy these marine ecosystems, they stop storing carbon, and instead release it back into the atmosphere, adding to the greenhouse gases that are emitted from fossil fuel burning. What's more, increased levels of carbon dioxide are leading to acidification of the oceans and reducing the ability of many species and habitats to survive. This in turn diminishes the capacity of oceans to buffer us against some of the worst impacts of climate change.

One of the key solutions to reverse the collapse of marine ecosystems is to stop overfishing. Catching fish from the sea is not inherently damaging. But when fishing techniques destroy marine habitats, for example through bottom trawling, and when fish are taken faster than stocks can replenish, then fishing becomes a major problem. Overfishing is officially recognised as the most significant driver of declines in ocean wildlife. In acknowledgement of this, there was an EU-wide agreement to end overfishing in 2014. At last we had an agreement to set quotas for fish catches within sustainable limits.

However, each year governments argue against the scientific advice, and each year catches are allowed that are far bigger than what is advised as the maximum sustainable yield. In terms of catches exceeding scientific advice, Ireland is one of the worst offenders. The appetite for short-term returns is winning out against long-term sustainability, even though this means we will soon have very few fish left in the sea.

The most exciting thing about Marine Protected Areas (MPAs), which are described in the chapter entitled 'The Big Blue', is that the benefits spill over into surrounding waters, allowing marine life to rebound in far-reaching ways. Studies from around the world have shown that MPAs can boost fishery catches nearby. Protecting marine habitats allows biodiversity to make a comeback, gives fish stocks a chance to recover, and offers coastal communities better opportunities for sustainable fishing into the future.

Ireland, however, has been slow to establish MPAs. The state had committed to allocating 10 per cent of our ocean territory as MPAs by 2020, though we missed that target by a country mile. At the time of publication, Ireland has less than 2.5 per cent of marine waters protected, one of the poorest records in Europe. A new internationally agreed target of 30 per cent MPAs by 2030 has now been set. Ireland has much to do to achieve this.

The Good News with the Bad

The examples I've chosen of biodiversity decline – in grasslands, peat bogs and the sea – highlight how all is far from rosy when it comes to the political appetite for nature protection in Ireland. These examples illustrate how short-term profit and the ruthless pursuit of economic growth dwarf conservation efforts.

Over and over, industry lobby groups and politicians knowingly allow continued relentless exploitation of natural resources, even though the consequences are devastating. This is bad news, and it is difficult to write, to hear about, and to read. But without acknowledging the scale of the challenge, we have little hope of changing the attitudes and economic systems to the extent that is required.

There is still time to turn these destructive trends around and to save many habitats and species from extinction. The approaches that work for nature are well known and recog-nised. It would not be difficult to ease the pressure on rivers and lakes by reducing nutrient pollution and dredging, so that salmon, eel and other aquatic organisms have a chance to recover. We could be allocating a far higher proportion of the already significant subsidies for agriculture towards results-based agri-environment schemes and other farmland conservation projects that are proven to help maintain species-rich grassland as well as other farmland habitats.

Through monitoring and research, huge strides have been made in recent years to better understand declines in biodiversity, both in Ireland and around the world. Effective actions include supporting communities through locally led conservation projects and committing educational resources, so that both the media and citizens are sufficiently informed to critically analyse the greenwashing that inundates us.

Implementing solutions, including practical actions and conservation policies, requires money, time, expertise and public support. Current financing commitments are not nearly enough to stem the loss of species and habitats, nor enough to embark on the necessary restoration of, for example, semi-natural grasslands, rivers, bogs, woodlands and sharks at sea, to name but a few.

We have passed the threshold of being able to ignore how climate breakdown and biodiversity collapse are undermining the viability of everything we depend upon. With enough momentum, there is still a possibility that downward trends can be reversed through landscape-scale ecosystem restoration.

It is our actions today that determine what the future holds.

Invitations to the Wild Embrace

🍄 Join Irish environmental non-governmental organisations (NGOs). The Irish Wildlife Trust, BirdWatch Ireland, An Taisce (the National Trust for Ireland) and the Irish Seed Savers Association are a few of the conservation charities through which committed nature enthusiasts, both professional and voluntary, work on behalf of Ireland's wild plants and animals. Most importantly, these NGOs advocate for stronger nature conservation policies. They need your support, your financial contributions, and the political clout that comes with large membership.

🍄 Give gifts to colleagues, family and friends of membership to Irish environmental NGOs. Membership often includes a subscription magazine filled with wildlife articles by local experts, campaign updates and lists of scheduled outings.

❦ Explore opportunities to connect with others who have an interest in protecting nature by attending events organised by conservation groups.

❦ Visit a bog where there is a raised walkway allowing access across the wet hummocks and pools. Look out for insect-eating sundew plants.

We can begin
to reimagine
the future

Taking Action

NOW that we find ourselves absorbed by the sweetness of ivy flowering in early winter; enchanted by the iridescent colours on a butterfly wing; lost in time examining lichen everywhere we look; and compelled to pause near long grass to listen out for grasshoppers, we may find that life is taking on a different hue. Familiar routes and places are no longer quite the same. There is far more depth and detail than we had previously assumed. Everything feels a little bit richer. Once we train ourselves to really see, the world is full of wonder.

As we cultivate our curiosity, we keep discovering the gazillion different ways that wild plants and animals have figured out how to live, with incredible adaptations and life cycles. Embracing nature, our values might shift a little. We might find that we are motivated to action. Once we begin to recognise nature's bounty, there follows an awakening that we each have a responsibility to care for the health of local habitats. With heightened awareness, we become attuned to the many tangible solutions that exist to environmental problems. We might be more inclined to work with others to get involved in community conservation projects.

In this frame of mind, we can begin to reimagine the future.

There are inspiring conservation initiatives underway across Ireland and the world. Learning from nature, people are turning towards greater symbiosis; managing the land with better balance; taking a long-time perspective; and caring for our environment with a sense of reverence and respect.

In Ireland, dozens of river trusts have sprung into existence in the last few years. Each trust is a broad community partnership working to restore healthy rivers. They are stabilising banks to prevent sediment from smothering salmon spawning grounds; removing invasive species; and working with local landowners to plant riparian woodlands that help prevent nutrients from seeping into waterways. With these kinds of community groups, positive action can be infectious.

Pioneering people have been restoring wild woodland ecosystems. Where grazing deer and goats are kept out, layers of life return, along with self-seeded saplings of wild sessile oak, downy birch, holly, willow and rowan. The 'Beara Rainforest' in west Cork is one such project, beautifully described in Eoghan Daltun's memoir, A*n Irish Atlantic Rainforest: A Personal Journey into the Magic of Rewilding*. Here Daltun charts the extraordinary journey of how a notion for restoration can grow into a powerful and inspiring legacy.

Beginning in 2009, Daltun removed substantial stands of invasive rhododendron and protected the woodland from feral goats and sika deer, who had reduced the ground flora to practically zero and killed many of the trees by stripping the bark from the trunks. In just a decade, these restorative actions have begun to deliver spectacular results. An explosion of luxuriant growth and a thriving Atlantic rainforest ecosystem now occupies what only 20 years ago was a severely degraded woodland. This project offers hope for native woodlands, both those already existing and those yet to exist.

In the Burren, semi-natural limestone grasslands are being actively managed to ensure the continuation of the area's incredibly rich biodiversity, so that rare butterflies, solitary bees, anthills and much else besides can survive into the future. The unique Burren practice of winter grazing on upland pastures is now encouraged through 'results-based' financial incentives, rewarding higher payments to farmers with the most biodiverse meadows.

This novel results-based approach, developed in response to mounting environmental challenges in the Burren, is a collaboration between farmers and ecologists. Not only has it been successful in preventing the loss of many precious Burren grassland habitats, but it has also inspired the roll-out of similar approaches to grassland conservation all over Ireland and further afield across the EU.

The 'Natura 2000' network of protected areas is a major

nature conservation initiative operating across Europe. It is the largest coordinated network of protected areas in the world. Many of the richest ecological sites are included, from salt marshes, mudflats and sand dunes to lakes, species-rich pastures and peat bogs, designated as 'Special Areas of Conservation' (SACs) and 'Special Protection Areas' for birds (SPAs).

Together with the EU's Birds Directive and Habitats Directive, which provide the legal framework for protecting the most vulnerable and threatened species and habitats, the Natura 2000 network is the backbone of biodiversity protection across Europe. There have been massive challenges to implementing these protective measures in Ireland, but without their crucial lifelines for biodiversity, much more would be lost. Properly implementing conservation laws and restorative measures are the most important things we can do to support nature in Ireland right now.

Marine habitats are increasingly a focus for ecological restoration. A coalition of scientists and conservation organisations have come together to pursue the designation and protection of Marine Protected Areas (MPAs) in at least 30 per cent of Ireland's ocean territory. (For a reminder of the importance of MPAs, refer back to the chapter entitled 'The Big Blue'.) This is an international target that has been set in international law, which many countries across the world are aiming for. If implemented meaningfully, and combined with effective controls to ensure sustainable fishing, MPAs can help breathe life back into parts of the ocean.

From each of these examples, there is a common theme. Giving nature space to recover allows ecosystems to nurture themselves back to bountiful, healthy states. Fostering abundant healthy habitats, on land, in water and out at sea, is the only hope we have of sustaining healthy and prosperous human civilisations, especially in a world being transformed by climate change.

Every community that comes together to effect change, from the ground up, is an essential component of the transition that is needed. Every sustainable job that is created, every bog that is restored, every garden that is mindfully cultivated, every tonne of carbon that is kept from the atmosphere – all are essential components of the changes that are needed.

Rewilding

Humans have now sprawled our influence over every part of the natural world. There is literally nothing left in Ireland that we could call true wilderness. Here and globally, the current food system is depleting nature at an astonishing rate. Today, we are living in a world in which farmed animals, mainly cows and pigs, account for 60 per cent of all mammals on the planet by weight. Humans comprise 36 per cent by weight. Wild animals make up just 4 per cent.[38]

One way to reverse the damage done and create resilience

for the future is to return large areas of land to wild nature. The eminent biologist E.O. Wilson (1929–2021) began a movement based on a principle that: 'Only by setting aside half the planet in reserve, or more, can we save the living part of the environment and achieve the stabilization required for our own survival.'

In Ireland, a sensible first step towards restoring nature is to facilitate ecological restoration in state-owned national parks. 'Rewilding' is where we allow natural processes to lead the way, giving species and habitats the space they need to recover. Rewilding is also a powerful means of helping us to reassess and reformulate our personal and cultural relationships with nature. Rewilding projects are being undertaken all over the world, offering hope for the future.

The results of restoration of Caledonian forest in the Scottish Highlands, begun twenty years ago, have exceeded expectations. By tackling overgrazing, tall heather becomes established again, which in turn encourages pioneer trees such as birch, rowan and willow. These trees bring up nutrients from the soil, allowing other trees such as pine, oak, ash and elm to grow. This process re-establishes ecological relationships, supporting interdependent webs of life across whole mountain ranges, from fungal mycorrhiza to majestic birds of prey.

When large-scale ecological restoration is implemented, peat bogs can switch from being carbon sources to carbon sinks. Improvements in water quality will mean healthier rivers and more bountiful fisheries, including the return of wild salmon and trout. Native woodland can recover and be allowed to expand across landscapes. Birds such as merlins, jays, woodpeckers, ospreys and golden eagles will return.

In Ireland, the Wild Nephin National Park in north-west Mayo contains extensive areas of Atlantic blanket bog, commercial forestry plantations and hill sheep pasture amongst stunning mountain landscapes. To many people, such beautiful open swathes of dramatic hills and mountains look 'wild'. However, as with upland areas all over Ireland, most of the Nephin mountain ecosystems are severely degraded. Peatlands have been drained and planted with tree monocultures, and as a result, water quality in the rivers is poor, limiting the richness of aquatic life. Plans are afoot to restore large areas of Wild Nephin to healthy habitats: rewetting peatlands, removing invasive rhododendron, and re-establishing native woodlands where once they thrived. Accelerating such initiatives is urgent.

The rewilding movement is different to what's gone before, mainly because the scale is so much bigger than piecemeal ecological restoration projects. Rewilding is about implementing a vision for a positive future, engaging the imagination, and inciting enthusiasm. Ecosystem restoration on a landscape scale is also a powerful antidote to the despair that comes with acknowledging the scale of loss we are facing.

The Role of Culture

Habitat restoration and rewilding are essential practical actions. However, in order to change the destructive trajectory which we are speeding along, a fundamental cultural shift is also needed. Culture shapes our relationship with nature, and so culture will shape the future.

In Ireland, we have deep ties with the land and a powerful appreciation for nature. Our stories have always shaped our values, beliefs and customs: from the stories told by hunter-gatherer societies who lived here for 4,000 years, to the stories of conquest and power that enabled colonialism. It is the role of culture to now reframe the stories we tell and transform the values that determine the course of history.

The choices we make, the conversations we have, the art we produce, the events we plan, all of these contribute to our stories and, in turn, to our common cultural values. Each of us has a role in precipitating the massive cultural shift that is needed, which is already permeating the undercurrents of our culture. We must begin to see the world anew, and to reconsider our place in nature. Each of us can work with our own personal strengths and abilities to contribute to a new narrative, and enact fresh approaches to nature that are engaging, joyful and rewarding.

Our well-being, both psychological and material, depends on healthy ecosystems, and our degree of conscious contact with them. Celebrating these connections is integral to creating a more hopeful future for wild nature, and for the viability of all that we know and love.

Further Reading

Wildflower Guides

I use *The Wild Flower Key: How to Identify Wild Flowers, Trees and Shrubs in Britain and Ireland*, by Francis Rose (first published Frederick Warne, 1981, latest edition 2006). This guide is widely considered the best of its kind for its combination of meticulous illustrations and the use of keys to aid plant identification.

The Wildflowers of Ireland: A Field Guide by Zoë Devlin (Gill Books, 2021) is a super guide for beginners because the plants are grouped by the colour of their flowers, making it quite user-friendly; plus it is specific to Ireland.

Ireland's Wild Orchids by Brendan Sayers and Susan Sex (Collins Press, 2013) is a beautiful little book with great descriptions of each native orchid and wonderful illustrations by botanical artist Susan Sex.

The Wild Flowers of Ireland by Declan Doogue and Carsten Krieger (Gill & Macmillan, 2010) is a big book packed with superb photographs and detailed descriptions of all the habitats you'll find across Ireland; a gem of a book.

Foraging Guides

Food for Free by Richard Mabey (first published in 1972 by Collins Press, reissued and updated many times, most recently 2012) is a classic foraging guide to over 200 types of food that can be gathered and picked in the wild, covering herbs, flowers, fruits, nuts, fungi and more.

The River Cottage Handbook: Hedgerow by John Wright (Bloomsbury Publishing, 2018) is a beautifully produced British book with pictures and recipes of many common hedgerow plants. The mushrooms book in the same series is also an excellent introduction to edible wild mushrooms.

Forgotten Skills of Cooking by Darina Allen (Kyle Cathie, 2009) contains many excellent insights and traditional Irish recipes for wild foraged foods.

Irish Seaweed Kitchen by Prannie Rhatigan is a wonderful guide and recipe book, as is the follow-up, Prannie Rhatigan's *Irish Seaweed Christmas Kitchen* (both Inishmurray Ink Publishing, 2018). The accompanying small, ring-bound, laminated booklet is ideal for bringing on seaweed foraging excursions and has a QR code for further information about each of the seaweeds described.

Insect Guides

Insects of Ireland by Stephen McCormack, Eugenie Regan and Chris Shields (Gill & Macmillan, 2012) is a must-have for insect enthusiasts; a comprehensive, compact guide to over 120 of Ireland's most popular insects, including all Irish species of butterflies, bumblebees, dragonflies, ladybirds, grasshoppers and shield bugs.

The Irish Butterfly Book by Jesmond Harding (self-published, 2022) is a fascinating comprehensive account with excellent illustrations, compiled with great care and the knowledge of 25 years of study. It contains practical tips for gardeners, too, and has its own YouTube channel (linked to within the book) to enjoy film footage of Ireland's butterflies.

Birds and Bird Guides

Irish Birds by David Cabot (HarperCollins, 2021) is an easy-to-use, illustrated colour guide in which birds are grouped together according to where they are most likely to be seen: in gardens, parks and buildings; farmland and hedgerows; woodland and scrubland; moorland and uplands; and freshwater or coastal areas, with background information about each of these habitats.

The Birds of Ireland by Jim Wilson and Mark Carmody (Gill & Macmillan, 2013) is a user-friendly photographic identification guide.

Birdwatching in Ireland with Eric Dempsey by Eric Dempsey (M.H. Gill & Company, 2011) will make you laugh out loud; a wonderful insight into a birder's world that covers identification and good places to visit as well as explaining bird physiology and behaviour.

Seaside Guide

Ireland's Seashore: A Field Guide by Lucy Taylor and Emma Nickelsen (Gill & Macmillan, 2018) is a superb small book that will help you to identify coastal plants, seaweeds, lichens, crabs, sponges, starfish, sea urchins, fish and more.

General Books about Nature in Ireland

Ireland's Generous Nature: The Past and Present Uses of Wild Plants in Ireland by Peter Wyse-Jackson (Missouri Botanical Garden Press, 2014) is an encyclopaedic and highly detailed account of the ethnographic uses of trees and plants, containing fascinating descriptions of how plants have been used in virtually every aspect of human life in Ireland: for food, clothes, dyes, folk remedies, medicine, construction, drinks, and human health and beauty.

An Irish Atlantic Rainforest: A Personal Journey into the Magic of Rewilding by Eoghan Daltun (Hachette Ireland, 2022) is a powerful, engaging and informative account of the rewilding of a 73-acre farm on the Beara Peninsula in west Cork; part memoir, part environmental treatise.

Diary of a Young Naturalist by Dara McAnulty (Milkweed Editions, 2021) is a joyful memoir by the then 15-year-old author about his love for the natural world, charting the seasons with richly evocative descriptions and personal narratives.

Whittled Away: Ireland's Vanishing Nature by Pádraic Fogarty (Gill & Macmillan, 2017) is an expertly written book about the devastation of Ireland's precious ecosystems by overfishing, industrial agriculture and pollution; a must read for anyone seeking a comprehensive account of how we've ended up in the state we're in, alongside solutions and possibilities for the future.

Our Wild World by Éanna Ní Lamhna (The O'Brien Press, 2021) is a lively discussion of ants, bees, spiders, whales, carbon footprints and mobile phones, all in Ní Lamhna's characteristically lively, witty style.

Online Resources

Wildflowers of Ireland website by Zoë Devlin is an excellent catalogue of over 800 flowering plants found in Ireland. http://www.wildflowersofireland.net/

The pollinators website associated with the All-Ireland Pollinator Plan by the National Biodiversity Data Centre is an exceptional online resource, with user-friendly guides to help identify bees and other pollinators, alongside planting lists, signage, posters and guidance for gardeners, businesses, schools, sports clubs, golf courses and more. https://pollinators.ie/

The National Biodiversity Data Centre makes biodiversity data and information more freely available to all, and provides information about citizen scientist initiatives across Ireland. A smartphone app allows people to enter sightings of biodiversity to contribute to national inventories. https://biodiversityireland.ie/

Endnotes

Opening to the Wild Embrace

1. In a meta-analysis, Mackay and Schmitt (2019) confirmed that there is a strong association between nature connection and positive environmental behaviour, as well as evidence that nature connection causes positive environmental behaviour. Additional references for this are cited in *Youth Knowledge and Perceptions of Climate Mitigation*, an Economic and Social Research Institute report, series number 153, November 2022, ESRI.

Connection

2. Attention Restoration Theory (ART) predicts that exposure to natural environments may lead to improved cognitive performance through restoration of a limited cognitive resource directed attention. ART posits that the mental fatigue associated with modern life is associated with a depleted capacity to direct attention. Results of a comprehensive review showed that working memory, cognitive flexibility and, to a less reliable degree, attentional control are improved after exposure to natural environments. See: Matt P. Stevenson, Theresa Schilhab and Peter Bentsen (2018) 'Attention Restoration Theory II: A Systematic Review to Clarify Attention Processes Affected by Exposure to Natural Environments', *Journal of Toxicology and Environmental Health*, Part B, 21:4, 227–268, DOI: 10.1080/10937404.2018.1505571

3. A. van den Berg, Y. Joyce and S. Koole (2016), 'Why Viewing Nature is More Fascinating and Restorative Than Viewing Buildings: A Closer Look at Perceived Complexity'. *Urban Forestry & Urban Greening*, 20, 397–401. https://doi.org/10.1016/j.ufug.2016.10.011

4. 'Spending at least 120 minutes a week in nature is associated with good health and well-being' by Mathew P. White, Ian Alcock, James Grellier, Benedict W. Wheeler, Terry Hartig, Sara L. Warber, Angie Bone, Michael H. Depledge and Lora E. Fleming. https://www.nature.com/articles/s41598-019-44097-3

5. While being in nature benefits human health, the diversity of natural environments also matters. Research has shown that there is a significant positive relationship between the richness of plant and bird species and the extent of positive impacts on mental health. See 'Species richness is positively related to mental health: a study for Germany', by Methorst et al, in *Landscape and Urban Planning*, Volume 211, 2021.

Reclaiming the Past

6. The first good archaeological evidence we have for settlement in the Mesolithic shows similarities in material use and buildings to that of northern England, suggesting that this is where Ireland's first people arrived from. The earliest known

evidence of human settlement in Ireland dates to 10,500 BC, although recent archaeological discoveries suggest that people had some presence here as early as 31,000 BC.

7. Personal communication with Professor Graeme Warren, associate professor in the School of Archaeology, University College Dublin, who specialises in the archaeology of hunter-gatherers and Mesolithic peoples of north-west Europe.

8. The first Neolithic people who came to Ireland are thought to have come from Scotland, as their buildings were similar to Scottish buildings of the same period.

9. In 1991 a mummified man was found in an Alpine glacier on the border between Italy and Austria. This ice-man, now known as Ötzi the Ice Mummy, lived 5,000 years ago. Around his neck was a leather thong containing chunks of birch polypore, a type of bracket fungus known to have an array of medicinal applications.

10. Some of the more famous of these Neolithic tombs include Newgrange, Knowth and Dowth in County Meath; Carrowmore and Carrowkeel in County Sligo; Lough Gur in County Limerick; and the Poulnabrone Dolmen in the Burren in County Clare.

Taming

11. The climax of woodland cover in Ireland spanned several thousand years, from 8,500 years ago to 5,900 years ago, when a wave of elm disease dramatically altered the woodland canopy, coinciding with the arrival of Neolithic people who made clearings in the woodland with stone axes.

What's in a Name?

12. The website Logainm.ie is a free resource for documenting the names of places in Irish, a first step to discovering the origin of the name of the townland where you live.

Hedgerows

13. Townland boundaries can be identified on the Ordnance Survey (OS) maps from 1839 to 1842 and subsequent Ordnance Survey maps. There is a very useful Ordnance Survey Ireland (OSI) National Townland and Historical Map Viewer available online, which also shows features such as springs, woodlands, marshes, mills, millraces and more.

14. Lichens are a joint venture between a fungus and an algae, so technically, they are classified among the kingdom of fungi rather than the kingdom of plants.

The Small Majority

15. Technically, insects don't hibernate, rather they go into a state of dormancy that is called 'diapause'.

Symbiosis

16. Symbiosis includes parasitism (when one organism is dependent on a host which it harms but does not directly kill); commensalism (when one species lives in or on another which it neither helps nor harms); and mutualism (an intimate coexistence of two species that benefits both).

17. Mycorrhiza comes from the Greek for 'fungus root'.

18. Much of this work has been brought to the fore by Professor Suzanne Simard in the University of British Colombia Faculty of Forestry, whose research is described in her book *Finding the Mother Tree*.

19. Many species of fungi don't produce mushrooms at all, existing entirely underground.

Luminous Woodlands

20. Shrews, mice and other small mammals produce high-pitched sounds that are above the frequencies that humans can hear. These creatures make sounds to communicate with one another, to attract mates, to hunt, and even to navigate using echo-orientation.

21. In Ireland, only peatlands, fens, saltmarshes and sand dunes are naturally open, treeless habitats.

22. According to the National Parks and Wildlife Service, about 85,000 hectares of native woodland exist in Ireland, about 1.25 per cent of the land area of the country.

23. The European average of tree cover is 36 per cent. No other EU country has a comparable reliance on the monocultures of exotic conifers that are so prevalent in Ireland.

Flowing Water

24. Only 53 per cent of rivers are in satisfactory ecological health, according to the monitoring work carried out by the Environmental Protection Agency under obligation to the Water Framework Directive. Nitrogen pollution is on the rise in nearly half of Irish rivers, representing a 30-fold increase on pre-2015 trends for nitrates, when only a tiny proportion of sites were showing increases.

25. Almost half of Irish rivers are failing to meet mandatory water quality requirements, officially called 'good status' in the EU Water Framework Directive. Nitrogen pollution is increasing, and currently, measures to reverse these trends are inadequate.

Life in the Air

26. Humans also have magnetite in their noses, especially those with the genetic lineage of long-distance migrations, such as Australian aboriginals. Through evolution, we have distanced ourselves from the ability to use our magnetic 'sense'.

Urban Nature

27. From the results of an EPA/Red C poll to measure attitudes towards the environment, incorporated in the EPA's report *2020 in Review.*

28. Each year, there are over 1,300 premature deaths in Ireland caused by poor air quality, specifically because of fine particles in our air. The main sources of this particulate matter are the same as Ireland's main sources of carbon emissions: transport, home heating and intensive agriculture.

29. Guidance for establishing habitats such as long meadows can be found on pollinators.ie, the website of the *All-Ireland Pollinator Plan.*

Nature at Nighttime

30. Circadian rhythm is the natural sleep–wake cycle that generally repeats every 24 hours.

Bearing Witness

31. Many curlews from more northerly latitudes travel to Ireland at the end of summer to spend the winter along our coastlines. Their beautiful call is often heard, but they should not be confused with the resident breeding population of curlews whose numbers are in such drastic decline.

32. 'Semi-natural' grasslands are the result of millennia of human activity altering the predominantly wooded landscape that existed naturally in Ireland thousands of years ago.

33. In just one six-year period, from 2010 to 2016, almost a third of all calcareous grasslands in Ireland were lost and over a quarter of lowland hay meadows.

34. Where once the fodder was grown locally, as part of diverse farm systems with both tillage and pastureland, globalisation and decreased transport costs have reduced the need for home-grown fodder as it can be imported from other regions. Ireland imported approximately 5.1 million tonnes of animal feed in 2018, largely from North and South America.

35. *A National Biodiversity Expenditure Review for Ireland* by R. Morrison and C. Bullock (UCD, 2018) states that Irish and EU government spending on agricultural supports is linked to trends towards increased intensification or specialisation, which has implications for habitats, water quality and species dependent on traditional or low-intensity farming.

36. A special report from the European Court of Auditors released in June 2020 called *Biodiversity on Farmland* reveals how the CAP has not halted the decline of biodiversity on farmland, and describes how €66 billion of CAP money over the 2014–2020 period has not delivered for biodiversity.

37. Raised bogs began to develop 10,000 years ago in the basins of shallow lakes left behind by retreating glaciers. A healthy raised bog is actively growing, with the surface slightly higher than the surrounding countryside (hence its name). Raised bogs are mainly in the midland counties of Ireland. Blanket bogs on the other hand are generally found in upland areas and along wet Atlantic coastal areas. On a blanket bog, abundant rainfall creates the conditions for acid peat to spread out to form a blanket covering huge areas of wet land.

Taking Action

38. *Food System Impacts on Biodiversity Loss*: research paper by Chatham House/United Nations Environment Programme, February 2021 (ISBN: 978 1 78413 433 4)

Index

Acknowledgements

A massive thank you!

To those who have inspired, encouraged and guided my interest in Ireland's wondrous natural world: Sarah and James McLoughlin; Gareth Bareham; Anne Behan (1959–2004); Declan Doogue; Éanna Ní Lamhna; and Seán Óg O'Dalaigh.

Thanks to my publisher Ciara Considine of Hachette Ireland for enthusiastically and expertly guiding the development of this work; and to Adrienne Murphy, who has been a knowledgeable and encouraging editor. I am also grateful to Sharon Bowers who has been generous with her support, time and advice.

Thank you to the good friends who have been fun and curious accomplices on many adventures in Ireland's wild outdoors over the years: Sarah Souther for her constant reminders that adventure and joy are everywhere; Amy McLoughlin (Carswell) for her steadying friendship and strength; Karen Smith for kindness and encouragement; Rhob Cunningham for his unnerving attachment to positivity; and Tina Dolan for perfectly timed insights. I am also grateful to dear friends Paula Kehoe; Lisa O'Neill; Bernie Pháid; Brían McGloinn; Karen Dolan; Keith, Eoghan, Ferdiad and Tess O'Reilly; Anja Nicholson; Paul Murphy; Stina Sandstrom; and Benny McLaughlin.

I am grateful to my family and extended family: Fiona Herbst; Juliet Herbst; Orson Herbst and Hilary McNamara; Pauline McNamara; Myles O'Reilly and Aideen Macken; Norma and John Macken; and my wonderful nieces and nephews. Thanks also to the west Cavan neighbours who have always been so open, kind and generous.

Thank you to all those, past and present, working for nature conservation in Ireland, including many former colleagues in the Irish Wildlife Trust, An Taisce – the National Trust for Ireland, BirdWatch Ireland and the wider ENGO community. Within the sector are a great many committed groups and individuals dedicated to speaking the truth, exposing ecocide and running conservation projects amid challenging circumstances. This work fosters hope for the future of Ireland's wild species and habitats.

Thank you to the *Eco Eye* team (Marcus Stewart, Killian McLoughlin, Raja Nundlall, Marc O'Gleasain, Louise O'Gallagher and Duncan Stewart) for their commitment to making great television programmes that tell important stories. Our filming trips each year are always fun and inspiring, and I learn so much from those we meet along the way. Writing *Nature File* and making documentaries for RTÉ lyric fm these past few years has also allowed me to indulge my curiosity about every conceivable aspect of nature in Ireland. Thanks to Sinéad Wylde, Eoin O'Kelly and all the team for this opportunity.

Thanks also to everyone who has permitted me to quiz them endlessly and been generous in sharing their understandings and shaping my thinking.